Makers of the Modern Theological Mind

Bob E. Patterson, Editor

Makers of the Modern Theological Mind
Bob E. Patterson, Editor

HANS KÜNG

John Kiwiet

HENDRICKSON PUBLISHERS
PEABODY, MASSACHUSETTS 01961-3473

HANS KÜNG

Copyright © 1985
Hendrickson Publishers, Inc.
P.O. Box 3473
Peabody, Massachusetts 01961-3473
All rights reserved.
Printed in the United States of America

ISBN 0-943575-64-8

Library of Congress Cataloging-in-Publication Data

Kiwiet, John.
   Hans Küng / by John Kiwiet.
      p. cm.
   Reprint. Originally published: Waco, Tex.: Word Books,
c1985. (Makers of the modern theological mind).
   Includes bibliographical references.
   ISBN 0-943575-64-8
   1. Küng, Hans, 1928-   . 2. Catholic Church—Doctrines—
History—20th century.   I. Title. II. Series:
Makers of the modern theological mind.
[BX4705.K76K58   1991]
230'.3'092-dc20   90-29870
                                                              CIP

To
Margaret
and
Eva, Henry, Talitha, Peter, and *Nicolina*

Contents

Editor's Preface

Who are the thinkers that have shaped Christian theology in our time? This series tries to answer that question by providing a reliable guide to the ideas of the men who have significantly charted the theological seas of our century. In the current revival of theology, these books will give a new generation the opportunity to be exposed to significant minds. They are not meant, however, to be a substitute for a careful study of the original works of these makers of the modern theological mind.

This series is not for the lazy. Each major theologian is examined carefully and critically—his life, his theological method, his most germinal ideas, his weaknesses as a thinker, his place in the theological spectrum, and his chief contribution to the climate of theology today. The books are written with the assumption that laymen will read them and enter into the theological dialogue that is so necessary to the church as a whole. At the same time they are carefully enough designed to give assurance to a Ph.D. student in theology preparing for his preliminary exams.

Each author in the series is a professional scholar and theologian in his own right. All are specialists on, and in some cases have studied with, the theologians about whom they write. Welcome to the series.

Bob E. Patterson, Editor
Baylor University

Preface

On 19 March 1978, Küng's fiftieth birthday was celebrated with great anticipation. After twenty years of conflict with the hierarchy, initially in Rome and later in Germany, Küng seemed to be on the winning side. A few weeks before, one of his colleagues, Dr. Walter Jens, had collected and published all the documents relevant to Küng's conflict with the bishops and had provided it with an eloquent introduction comparing Küng's situation with one of Kafka's scenes. On the morning of March 19 Küng had mailed a copy of his second major work, *Does God Exist?*, to the German Bishops Conference. A third exciting volume was presented by the staff of Küng's research center. It was a concise and comprehensive survey of *Hans Küng: His Work and His Way*, which is still the best short introduction to this controversial theologian.

There was only one dissonant note on that exciting morning. The popular illustrated magazine *Der Spiegel* (The Mirror) had published a very critical article in which Hans Küng was accused of harboring a martyr's complex; the article stated that his presumed conflict was mere ostentation for the sake of gaining popularity, and that most of his supposedly revolutionary statements were not really anything new. The article was a complete turnabout from earlier articles by the same magazine which had lauded Küng as the contemporary

Catholic hero following the steps of the great reformer Martin Luther. Our visit that morning with Küng was overwhelmed by the excitement of the new publications and by the sudden rejection by the secular press. It introduced us, however, in a vivid manner to the controversy surrounding Hans Küng. It is a question whether Küng himself was consciously aware of all the antagonistic forces he had evoked. In Chapter VI of this study we will be introduced to those parties in the Church of whom Küng was aware—the bishops, the social activists, the monastic orders, and especially the Vatican canon lawyers.

As someone at home in Reformation history I was really challenged to meet this modern-day Luther. Among obvious differences there were striking parallels. I gladly took upon myself the study of Küng's multitudinous books and articles covering a wide range of issues. Ever since Vatican II beginning in the year 1962 I had followed closely the developments in the Catholic Church and Hans Küng provided a dramatic sequel. He placed his position and honor upon the line for bringing into practice the ideals uttered during the first year of Vatican II. It would have been quite a transformation if the Catholic Church had followed the lead of Pope John XXIII! Other forces, however, stemmed the tide of change, and Vatican II became merely a memorable event in Catholic life and worship.

Küng will remain, however, a rich resource for Catholics and Protestants for the contemporary issues of ecclesiology, ethics, and philosophy. His proposals may be controversial but they are addressing the current status of the issues involved. As preacher and lecturer Küng still draws large crowds—and he is much in demand as contributor to magazines, journals and news programs. He defies our classifications of conservative or liberal, of evangelical or mainline Protestant, of progressive or charismatic Catholic. Each of these modalities in Christianity can find a point of identity with Küng even though at other points he is different from them.

One can not follow the trail of Küng without the help of guides along the way. Küng's associates, Hermann Häring and Karl-Joseph Kuschel, were quite helpful in getting me oriented in the library of the Institute for Ecumenical Research in Tübingen. I have great appreciation for the librarians and Catholic colleagues in the universities of Nijmegen, Tilburg and Utrecht for their willingness to respond to sometimes vague questions. The year of sabbatical study provided by Southwestern Baptist Theological Seminary in Fort Worth, Texas, was of crucial importance for this project.

After I returned home from the experiences abroad the actual work had to be done among numerous other responsibilities. I am greatly indebted to my wife, Margaret, and to our children for their encouragement and patience in times when I was too much absorbed by the subject matter of this research. I am grateful to students who chose this material for their papers and to colleagues willing to listen and discuss. Miss Angela Double, my secretary, is to be mentioned for typing major sections of my often illegible manuscript. Finally, Dr. Bob Patterson and Word Publishers are to be commended for their patience in waiting for a text long overdue. The delay in publication has allowed us, at least, to report on the outcome of Küng's conflict with his superiors. May this publication be a genuine asset to the series of the "Makers of the Modern Theological Mind."

John J. Kiwiet

I
Emerging Leadership

1. The Formative Years, 1928–1955

Later biographers may want to analyze the psycho-social influences that engendered the provocative leader in Roman Catholic life and thought, the Rev. Dr. Hans Küng. They may point to Switzerland as the cradle of Western democracy and the champion for political and religious freedom. They may refer to the scenic town of Sursee, fourteen miles northwest of Lucerne where Küng grew up among a population of Protestants and Catholics. They will study the middle-class merchant family that, for two generations, had been in the shoe trade. They may make psychological observations concerning the role of Küng as the eldest son in a family of five sisters and one brother; they may also draw a profile of his parents, Hans and Emma (Gut) Küng, who with pride and devotion introduced their son into the Catholic faith.[1] The mature scholar, devoted pastor, and eloquent speaker, Hans Küng, reflected the urge for freedom, the sense of pride, and the intimate devotion worthy of his background. It must have been quite supportive to Küng when, during a conflict situation with Rome, twenty thousand signatures from the Lucerne area assured him of the loyalty of his Catholic compatriots.[2]

Leaving these familiar surroundings behind was the first step to

personal distinctiveness. At high school age, Küng went to the city
of Lucerne where he matriculated in a coeducational Latin school.
The daily interaction with Protestants, Jews, and fellow Catholics
opened his eyes to common concerns, as the scholarly dialogues
with Protestant and Jewish theologians in later years demonstrated.
The introduction into the Greek classics, in art and literature, taught
him how to evaluate the spirit of modern secular man. In retrospect,
Küng considered the years in Lucerne a widening of his horizons
from a traditional dogmatic outlook to a progressive vision of church
and society.[3] In spite of a cumulation of impressions, the young
student proved himself to be a diligent pupil. In later years, he
mastered a speaking knowledge of eight languages in addition to
his mother tongue, German.[4] With his blue eyes and blond wavy
hair, he must have been a popular youngster. As a genuine Swiss,
he grew to like skiing and swimming. Still today, Küng is a sporty,
slim, and well-groomed parson often in striking contrast with his
Italian dark and short colleagues.

By the time of his graduation in 1948, Küng was confronted
with the alternative of either continuing his education in the humanities or taking up his earlier religious aspirations. Küng decided for
the latter course without any parental pressure; as he later stated:
"I went to Rome completely voluntary and in full knowledge of
what lay in store for me there." [5] In contrast to the liberality of
his teenage years, Küng chose consciously for the disciplined spirituality of a Jesuit environment in the center of his religion, the sacred
city of Rome. He found lodging in the German College and matriculated at the Pontifical Gregorian University, which both are under
the auspices of the Jesuit order. At the age of twenty, he found
himself in the center of the ecclesiastical arena, where he would
carry on his gladiatorial fight until this very day.

Like millions before him, Küng was deeply impressed by the
splendor and immensity of the ecclesiastical capital of Roman Christianity. With awe and admiration, he must have traced the steps
of St. Francis, Erasmus, and Luther through the streets and churches
of old Rome. When, in later years, he wrote a critical analysis of
the Church, Küng still could not refrain from eulogizing the great
city of the popes. With approval, he quoted Macaulay who, even
as a non-Catholic, was of the opinion that "the proudest royal houses
are but of yesterday, when compared with the line of the Supreme

Pontiffs." Küng himself praised Rome as "the blend of venerable age and vigorous youth, a powerful organization, sprung from humble roots, spread throughout the world, with hundreds of millions of adherents and a strictly ordered hierarchy. . . ." [6]

The stately leadership of Pope Paul XII was at the height of its power and fame. Thousands of pilgrims journeyed to Rome during the year 1950, which had been proclaimed a holy year. On 1 November of that year, the pope solemnly proclaimed the first and only dogma since 1870 of the assumption of Mary, even without a council in session. From the balcony of the Vatican palace on St. Peter's square, Pope Pius XII declared boldly: "Our voice, which by the help of the Spirit confirmed the unique distinction of the heavenly mother, is the voice of the centuries, we may even say, the voice of eternity." [7]

Unlike Erasmus and Luther, the zealous ministerial student, Küng, absorbed these impressions without question. The new dogma seemed to him "a suitable expression of the Catholic understanding of the faith." [8] In debate with fellow students, he rejected their criticism of his German professors of theology as pride and negativism. Küng had no interest in the liberal views of his older colleagues; he rather subjected himself conscientiously to the strict rules of the German College. [9] The Spiritual Exercises of Ignatius of Loyola became, next to the New Testament, the most influential book for Hans Küng. According to his own testimony, Loyola's exercises conveyed to him three abiding norms: the will of God in all situations of life, the person of Christ as the concrete exemplification of God's will, and a life of "active indifference." [10] In his later writings, Küng described this lifestyle as an indifference for the things of this world, like money and possessions. It was a lifestyle, however, of active involvement in life's concerns, never for the purpose of power or control, but always for the sake of service to mankind on behalf of God's will in Christ.

Within the context of this religious devotion, a diverging intellectual development began to mark the young student. While the masses of pilgrims marched through the streets of Rome during the holy year, Küng increasingly concentrated on expressions of atheistic humanism for his studies at the Gregorian University. In the year 1951, Küng received his licentiate degree in philosophy under Alois Naber based upon a thesis on the existentialist, Jean Paul Sartre. [11]

Küng would always maintain a fascination for those who defied Christianity. In his book on the question, *Does God Exist?*, Küng described and evaluated the atheists—Feuerbach, Karl Marx, Nietzsche, and Sigmund Freud—as "prophets" of Western culture.[12] They taught Christians and non-Christians alike a sense of realism, which Küng discovered also in the Scriptures. In spite of his love for his Jesuit teachers, Küng soon developed a sense of criticism for their Neo-Thomistic speculative theology. In contrast to abstract speculation, Küng would later on search for a biblical realism open to the actual needs of man.

In the emerging conflict of thought the young student received constructive guidance from his spiritual supervisor, Father Wilhelm Klein. In response to Küng's searching mind, Father Klein focused his attention on the German philosopher, George Hegel, and on the Swiss Reformed theologian, Karl Barth.[13] Küng became so impassioned by Barth's theology that he decided to stay in Rome four more years to gain a licentiate in theology. In the year 1955, he successfully defended a thesis on Barth's doctrine of justification. Two years later, Küng earned a doctor's degree on the same subject at the Catholic Institute in Paris.[14] The study on Barth became a launching pad for Küng's spectacular career as an author and a theologian. Father Klein's other suggestion, concerning the philosopher Hegel, took several years to materialize.[15] In a simplified fashion, one can say that Küng's first fifteen years of publication [16] moved from Barth to Hegel and from a theocentric theology to a Christocentric theology. This move from revelational theology to empirical dialectic thought coincides with the transition to biblical realism mentioned above.

In retrospect, Küng stated that "the fundamental decisions did not, as is often believed, take place in Paris or in Germany, but in Rome." [17] By the use of the term "decisions," Küng referred to his emerging outlook on life and to his judicious acceptance of the Church. His own potentialities called him to pastoral as well as to educational ministry. He served as chaplain to the Italian employees of his college,[18] while he also was chairman of several academic work groups.[19] Pastoral care and theological concern would gradually merge into a genuine pastoral theology as one finds demonstrated in Küng's bestseller, *On Being a Christian* (1976).[20]

One of the more personal experiences during the completion of his time in Rome was Küng's ordination to the priesthood in October 1954.[21] Surrounded by his grateful parents, brother, and five sisters, and his friends and superiors, Küng became "Father" for the faithful in the prestigious church of Saint Peter in Rome. Even though Küng in later years never laid claim to his ordination, but rather demanded attention for his critical insights, he must have experienced a sense of achievement and of being accepted by the universal Catholic Church as a minister and a leader.

When he left Rome after his promotion to the degree of Licentiate in Theology in the spring of 1955, he had concluded a period of gradual discovery of the ideological forces within as well as outside of the Church. His studies on Barth, Hegel, and Sartre had familiarized him with Protestant theology, with dialectic philosophy, and with secular existentialism. When his Church changed its attitude a few years later from an exclusive to an inclusive approach to non-Catholic ideologies, Küng would be ready to take upon himself a role of leadership in that era of transition known as the era of Vatican II.

2. The Parisian Years, 1955–1957

An added significance of the years in Rome were Küng's frequent encounters with Catholic leaders from various parts of the world. During the evening hours, they would present and discuss the basic issues of the Church with the residents of the German College.[22] One of these visiting scholars made an abiding impression on Hans Küng. It was the gentle Dominican Father, Yves Congar, who was in Rome just after the seminary of the French Worker Priests had been ordered closed by the Vatican in the summer of 1953. The leading scholars, the Fathers Congar and Chenu, had been discharged in a most inconsiderate manner. Küng recalls how he was deeply disturbed about these transactions and how they led contributed decisively to a "demythologization" of the angelic Pope Pius XII.[23]

The disillusion in Rome, his new connections with Congar and others, and the attraction of the vitality of the French Catholics caused Küng to complete his theological studies at the Catholic Institute in Paris. After seven years of rigid discipline in Rome, he experienced a feeling of enormous relief and liberation at his arrival in Paris. He was free to participate in cultural events and to enjoy the lectures at the Sorbonne, the University of Paris. For the first time in his life, Küng attended a seminar in New Testament exegesis, under the Protestant professor, Oscar Cullmann. Küng gained new insight in philosophy through the lectures of Professor Henri Gouhier, who was a specialist on Descartes and on seventeenth-century French philosophy.[24] The contrast between Descartes and Pascal was discussed and, consequently, became the subject material of Küng's first lecture at the University of Tübingen in the fall of 1960. The same contrast became a major theme in Küng's latest book on the question of the existence of God.[25] The influences of Paris have strengthened his search for realism; ultimately, the plight of secular man appeared more urgent to Küng than the search of ecclesiastical man for union and mutual understanding.

During his two years in Paris, Küng was engaged actively in broadening his horizons in the ecclesiastical territory as well. To this end, he spent time for short periods of study in Amsterdam, Berlin, Madrid, and London.[26] The Dutch Catholic Dominicans were involved in planning the controversial *Dutch Catechism;*[27] the Austrian Jesuit scholar, Karl Rahner, was engaged in extensive literary activities, which later on included close cooperation with Küng.[28] During a course at the Catholic Institute, Küng met the Jesuit priest, Gélineau, who had introduced congregational hymn-singing in the French Catholic Churches.[29] The *Dutch Catechism,* Rahner's literary activity, and French congregational singing were different aspects of a wave of renewal going through the West European Catholic Church. The word "renewal" would be mentioned frequently in Küng's second book on *The Council, Reform and Reunion* (1961).[30]

These avenues to renewal involved also the Dominican Father, Yves Congar, whom Küng had met in Rome. During the years in Paris, he learned about Congar's ecumenical concerns. It was while in Paris that Küng read the French edition of Congar's "True and False Reform in the Church," which had been refused permission to be translated into other languages by the Vatican in 1950.[31] Ever since the Reformation by Martin Luther, the concept of reform had been controversial for Catholic leadership. In a most careful manner, Father Congar suggested that the Church must always be willing to be reformed: "ecclesia semper reformanda." Furthermore, it was his firm conviction that real reform in the Church would include a reunion of all Christians. Such a reform was not to involve doctrine,

but would rather be a spiritual renewal expressing itself in reconciliation between Christians within and outside the Church.[32] "It is only
in the total communion of believers that the complete truth will be
found," was his firm conviction.[33]

With the ascendance of Pope John XXIII in 1958, Congar's concern received prime attention. A few months later an ecumenical
council was announced. Father Congar would play a leading role
and at his side would be the young theological advisor, Hans Küng.
His second major book, mentioned above, would have Congar's key-
words in its title, "reform" and "reunion." Küng's later books on
the Church reflected Congar's emphasis on a ministry of service
for priesthood and laity. According to Küng, Congar had, next to
Karl Barth, a major influence on his work.[34]

Later on in life, Küng would be involved in resistance against
Rome's leadership. It was in Paris that he had his first experiences
in critical evaluation of his Church and in polemics with its leaders.
France had been in tension with Rome ever since Charlemagne,
and the Conciliar movement of the fifteenth century had been a
continuing challenge to the centralist position of many popes. During
Küng's years in Rome, Pope Pius XII had issued the encyclical
"Humani Generis," which was directed partly against "certain false
opinions, which threaten to undermine the foundations of the Catholic
Church." This referred to a group of French Catholic theologians.[35]
The Swiss conservative Catholic theologian, Garrigou-LaGrange, had
labeled this French theological movement as the "New Theology." [36]

The new ideas originated from a Jesuit theological school in Lyon-
Fourvière, where the Fathers Henri de Lubac and Jean Daniélou
were promoting a more spiritual pastoral theology as a remedy against
the barren scholastic teachings of traditional theology. These fathers
were influenced by the like-minded Protestant theologians, Rudolf
Otto and Søren Kierkegaard. Like Erasmus, the "new theologians"
suggested a return to the Greek fathers of the early Church for a
fresh theological orientation. To this intent, they began publishing
a most extensive series of annotated texts of the Greek fathers, followed by an equally ambitious series of historical and theological
studies.[37]

Father de Lubac wrote two of the earliest volumes in the series
of theological monographs. He subjected the scholastic concept of
"pure nature" to a theological evaluation. As a result, he concluded

that this Aristotelian concept does not do justice to the concrete
terminology of the Scriptures. By disqualifying the term "nature,"
de Lubac hoped to clear a way for new avenues of thought concerning
discussions on the "nature of the Church," the "nature of man,"
and even on the "nature of Christ." [38] For Roman Catholic theologians, this approach meant an undermining of their supposedly un-
changeably formulated dogmas when the validity of traditional
terminology was questioned. Even though Küng did not think de
Lubac's issues were conclusive,[39] he used in later years the same
approach when arguing against the final validity of the Chalcedon
formulation or when he questioned the term infallibility in connection
with the pope. For Küng, the Spirit was to prevail over the letter
and the freedom of adjustment was to prevail over faithfulness to
tradition. At this point, Küng approached the Protestant conviction
that all councils, dogmas, and Church fathers were to be subjected
to the authority of the Scriptures.

Because of his identification with the "New Theology," the Swiss
Jesuit, Hans-Urs Von Balthasar, had requested to be laicized in 1950.
In his brilliant argument with Barth, he maintained that this theologian had rejected Catholicism on the basis of the mere scholastic
concept of "pure nature." In this discussion with Barth, Von Balthasar demonstrated that the Thomistic concept of the analogy of being
was not based on pure nature but rather on the sacramental nature
of man. God and world do not have a naturalistic commonality but
rather a communication of grace.[40] Since Von Balthasar acted as
Küng's senior friend,[41] it was greatly encouraging for Küng to observe
that Barth apparently accepted the arguments of Von Balthasar. According to Küng, after 1950, no reference to the analogy of being
is made any more, although Barth never conceded publicly that he
had changed his mind on this controversial issue.[42]

Küng's encounter with Barth was another highlight during the
years in Paris. After Küng had mailed his master's thesis to Barth,
he telephoned him. Barth's first question was: "Are you in fact an
old man or a young man?" [43] At this time, Küng was merely twenty-
seven and Barth sixty-nine; yet, a most amiable relationship resulted.
In his eulogy on Barth, Küng called his older colleague a "fatherly
friend," the same appellation he used for Father Yves Congar.[44]
This personal relationship was the decisive factor for Protestant reviewers of Küng's book on the concept of justification in Barth's

Dogmatics. It seemed most unusual that a conscientious Protestant theologian would appear to be so Catholic in his thought. Around his fiftieth birthday, Küng reminisced about his first explosive publication: "This was something nobody had thought possible, and without exaggerating it meant something like an ecumenical sensation." [45] Barth's introductory letter to Küng's publication stated, however unambiguously: "Your readers may first of all be assured, that you present me correctly and that my intentions are actually what you are inferring." [46] These words settled the issue for most reviewers.

Very little attention was given to questions that Barth raised at the end of his introduction, where he asked rhetorically: "How can it be explained, that all this could remain hidden for such a long time and for so many people inside as well as outside of the Church?" [47] Referring to the dogma of transubstantiation, the sacrifice of the mass, the position of Mary, and the infallibility of the pope, Barth seemed far from convinced that Protestantism and Romanism were mere variations of the same faith. He summarized his observations by the following picturesque remark: "Above all I welcome your book and consider it—as from the window of Noah's ark—another clear symptom, that the flood of recent times . . . is receding. . . ." Concluding with one of his many paradoxes, Barth stated that Protestants and Catholics were "separated in faith," yet within the context of "the same faith . . . in the same Lord." [48]

In Paris, on 21 February 1957, Küng defended his doctor's thesis on the concept of justification in Karl Barth. Hans Urs Von Balthasar, who initially had suggested the topic, came over from Basel to attend the formal occasion at the Catholic Institute. Louis Bouyer was the promoter, while Professor Guy de Broglie spoke in support of Küng's thesis.[49] Immediately after the promotion, a German translation was published with the approval of the bishop of Basel and accompanied by the above mentioned introductory letter of Karl Barth. Several negative reactions reached the Holy Office in Rome, so that a special file number was set up to coordinate the incoming criticisms on the young doctor of theology. Küng feared that his book would be placed on the index of forbidden books, but his former professors in Rome protected his thesis from crass misunderstandings. The once vigorous leadership of Pope Pius XII was waning and the matter at hand seemed too complex for an easy rejection.[50]

The years in Paris had been a most productive time during which the groundwork laid in Rome received concrete direction. With a few exceptions, all of Küng's later activities and publications can be explained as elaborations of the themes and questions encountered during the years in Rome and Paris. His recent and most voluminous book, *Does God Exist?*, harks back to these initial years even more intensely than previous publications. It demonstrated that for Küng the problems of secular man, symbolized by Paris, prevailed over the problems of religious man, symbolized by Rome.

3. The Years of Publicity, 1957–1984

For almost twenty-five years Küng has been in the public eye. Without the modern conveniences of communication and transportation, Küng could not possibly have been exposed to so many thousands of viewers, listeners, and readers. The publication on Hans Küng's work in 1978 listed 27 books translated into more than 150 non-German editions and 274 articles that have been translated for several international journals. There seemed to be no end to the public appearances, lectures, interviews, and dialogues. He was editor of theological studies and journals; [51] since 1964, he has been director of the Institute for Ecumenical Research in Tübingen, which was established to gather resource materials and to catalogue the innumerable documents related to his activities. These include minutes to meetings, reviews of his books, newspaper reports of his lectures, and his massive correspondence with friends and foes.[52]

What was Küng's appeal throughout these years? First of all, he is a controversialist causing a lively debate wherever he appears. His style of writing reflects a continuous thinking in polarities; while he claims the via media Küng leaves opponents to the right as well as to the left. His most popular work was the voluminous bestseller, *On Being a Christian*, in which he advocates neither a pietist nor a revolutionary position but rather a life of confident service. Related to this confrontational approach is his personal appeal. Küng is no slave of totalitarian institutions or of social custom, but rather presents himself primarily as a friend for each human being. His impressive research is matched by a series of theological meditations dealing with the reality of suffering, conflict, and frustration.[53] Robert McAfee Brown most adequately expressed this personalism in his open letter to Küng concerning the just mentioned publication: "You manage to confront us with that person, a real person, who really died, and whom you never etherialize into a phony kind of Christ." [54]

Controversiality and personal appeal were carried on the waves of history; the events of these waves coincided with the crucial years in Küng's life and popularity. The first concentration of events took place in the year 1959. The newly elected pope, John XXIII, electrified the Catholic hierarchy on 25 January of that year by announcing his desire for an expeditious ecumenical council. This would mean an open discussion of church policy and its relation to non-Roman Catholic Christians. No discussion about internal or external relations had taken place since the infamous council of 1870, now called Vatican I. With prophetic insight, Küng, who had been vicar of the First Catholic Church in Lucerne since his departure from Paris, held a sermon on the reunion with the "separated Christians" one week earlier, on 18 January. On the next day, he addressed the faculty and students of the University of Basel. Upon the invitation of Karl Barth, he spoke boldly on the subject, "Ecclesia semper reformanda," the topic introduced by Congar about ten years earlier. This presumably Calvinist slogan for the need of continual reform in the Church was in blatant contrast to the triumphalist spirit of the Counter Reformation in the Catholic Church up to that time.[55]

Küng was the man of the hour! The German Catholic leadership was greatly impressed with the young Swiss pastor-theologian. During the spring of 1959, Professor Hermann Volk invited Küng to become assistant professor for dogmatics at the Catholic faculty of the University of Münster. In the meantime, Küng immersed himself in the first writing project since his thesis. Within a few months, the manuscript was ready for the German edition of *The Council, Reform and Reunion* that covered the same territory as his preceding lecture in Basel.[56] The text was circulated among dignitaries and theologians in the Catholic Church; also, Karl Barth was asked about the delicate subject of a possible reunion of Rome and Reformation. Next to strong support, Küng elicited decisive opposition to his plea for reform and his hopes for reunion. Already in the fall of 1959, even before publication of his book, voices of protest were heard.[57]

Within a year after his arrival in Münster, Germany, Küng was appointed regular professor for systematic theology in the Catholic faculty of the prestigious University of Tübingen. He was to follow the progressive tradition of the nineteenth-century Catholic theolo-

gians, Adam Möhler and Ignatius Von Döllinger, who have both
been leading scholars in Tübingen. Little did Küng realize that ten
years later he would be involved in a similar conflict as Von Döllinger,
who was among the last ones to hold out against the proclamation
of the dogma of the infallibility of the pope in 1870. Unlike Von
Döllinger, Küng has remained faithful to the Roman Catholic Church,
where his predecessor was influential in starting the old Catholic
Church.[58]

The year 1959 was a year of great promise; eagerly, Küng accepted
speaking engagements to most of the Western European countries.
One of his popular addresses raised the question of the day: "Does
the Council come too early?" Of course, for the thirty-two-year-old
Küng the answer was: "No." Enthusiastically, he challenged his
audiences to follow the lead of the new pope, who had called for
an "aggiornamento," or an "opening of the windows," to let the
fresh air of a new day enter the Catholic community.[59]

The next wave of attention for Küng and the Catholic Church
was 1963. In October of the preceding year, the first annual session
of Vatican II had been opened by the eighty-year-old Pope John
XXIII. Küng had been invited as theological advisor by the end of
the first session and he became a welcome speaker for bishops from
every corner of the world. He was the youngest and most articulate
speaker in the venerable world of hierarchs and he was a favorite
resource person for press conferences.

As a result of this publicity, Küng made his first six-week tour
through the United States during the months of March and April
of 1963. Reactions to his lecture, "The Church and Freedom," were
enthusiastic, although vehemently critical by conservative Catholics.
The Catholic University of America in Washington, D.C., placed
an interdict on Küng's lectures, while the Catholic University of
St. Louis gave him an honorary doctor's degree. The popular President John F. Kennedy received him at the White House and Protestant scholars welcomed him as a new Luther.[60]

The year 1963 added a new dimension to the deepening conflict
between Küng and his opponents. Thus far, only the issues of justification, reform, and reunion with Protestants had been sensitive topics.
Now the structure of the Catholic Church itself was subjected to a
critical analysis. Küng had broached this subject in his inaugural
address for the University of Tübingen in 1960; he then had elabo-

rated upon it for a publication, which came out in May of 1962 under the title, *Structures of the Church*.[61] As Luther had done once before, Küng questioned the absolute authority of the councils and the so-called divine right of the pope to convene and preside over these councils.

A crucial development in this discussion was the encounter with his Protestant colleague, Ernst Käsemann. For the first time, said Küng, he had come in personal touch with a theologian using the radical historical critical method of Scripture interpretation. Küng was deeply touched by this new approach (for him). As a result, he "buried himself" in the relevant literature, according to his remark in a later interview.[62] Küng's publications would always take an intensive and critical recourse to the Scriptures after his encounter with Käsemann.[63]

A turning point in Küng's influence in Rome was the sudden death of Pope John XXIII on 3 June of this crucial year, 1963. Pope Paul VI vowed, indeed, to complete the plans of his predecessor, but he definitely wanted a more moderate policy. The second annual session of Vatican II meant an immediate change in Küng's position. The new Theological Commission was placed under the chairmanship of Cardinal Ottaviani, which caused Küng to refuse further participation in this Commission.

During this session of Vatican II, Küng was summoned to appear before a committee of the Holy Office, where he was requested to give account of his publication on the *Structures of the Church*. Through the benevolent influence of the chairman, Cardinal Bea, Küng was merely admonished to remain closer to the accepted teachings of the Catholic Church. In the initial days of the second session, Küng began his voluminous book on *The Church*. What he was not able to share in Commission would appear in print! There is a change in tone from enthusiastic allegiance to proud defiance of the Church of his fathers. Küng had been moved from the vanguard to the rear guard of the institutional Church.[64]

The change of direct influence did not hurt Küng's popularity, however; actually, the more intense the conflict with Rome became, the more extensive the news coverage became. Küng knew how to choose his moments of confrontation! Some reviewers have called him an editorialist for that very reason. On 18 July 1970 was the centennial commemoration of the promulgation of the dogma of infallibility. On that same day, Küng had his most controversial book published under the German equivalent of the title, *Infallible? An Inquiry.*[65] The Italian edition appeared one week earlier in order to get full attention of the celebrating cardinals, the pope, and the international press.

The content of this publication did not deal, however, with the centennial as such, but rather with the disturbing encyclical, *Humanae Vitae,* issued two years earlier. In a time of increasing concern for overpopulation of the world, Pope Paul VI had issued an affirmation of the 1930 encyclical prohibiting artificial birth control. From inside sources, Küng allegedly knew that the prestige of the pope was more at stake than the destiny of mankind. According to canon lawyers, a change of position on birth control would supposedly have meant a negation of the infallibility of earlier popes. This issue provided Küng with a concrete case for investigating and questioning the biblical and historical arguments in support of the controversial dogma of infallibility.[66]

Since the death of Pope John XXIII, regular conflicts between Küng and the hierarchy escalated up to the major eruption of 1970. It was painful for Küng to read the vehement criticism by his senior coeditor of the journal, *Concilium,* Karl Rahner. Without prior consultation, Rahner publicly denounced Küng as a "liberal Protestant" or a "sceptic philosopher."[67] Küng responded on the same level by qualifying Rahner's ideas as "textbook theology."[68] Then Rahner published a collection of articles by leading scholars who rejected Küng's position.[69] Küng gathered loyal colleagues and published their statements under the title, *Infallible, a Summation,* in response to Rahner.[70] In the meantime, Küng had been denounced by the German bishops and the Italian Commission of Faith. A complex interaction followed[71] until finally, in December 1979, Küng was relieved from his responsibilities as professor on behalf of the Roman Catholic Church, although he has maintained his secular contract with the University of Tübingen.[72] It is clear that the concept of infallibility was the most sensitive nerve in Catholic life and thought.

The gradual dissociation with the hierarchy and with his conservative Catholic colleagues made Küng a hero for progressive Catholics and Protestants. Between 1963 and 1980, Küng was engaged in ten major lecture tours of which five included the United States.[73] During the same period, he received four honorary doctor's degrees, two from Catholic universities and two from non-Catholic universities.[74] In the spring of 1968, Küng was a guest professor at the Union Theological Seminary in New York and, one year later, at the evangelical-theological faculty of the University of Basel.[75]

His lectures had an inflammatory effect on audiences. Küng described his objective graphically in a later interview: "the alarm had to sound." [76] Küng asserted that indirect and carefully formulated admonitions had been of no avail after the enthronement of Pope Paul VI and his successors. Even though at each occasion Küng would affirm his Catholic Christian faith, this clearly had to be distinguished from an endorsement of the Romanist policy of centralization. According to Küng, the universal Church does not need to prove itself by authoritarian power and absolute formulations of dogma. The Church should rather extend its witness by its presence and action in the world. "Remaining in the truth is more a matter of orthopraxy than of orthodoxy," wrote Küng in a concluding article on the infallibility of the Church.[77]

The tumultuous year of 1970 also saw the publication of Küng's delayed study on Hegel. It was the year of the bicentennial celebration of Hegel's birth. Among the several studies published for this occasion, Küng's work stood out for its detailed and extensive research. Hegel's dialectic thought provided the texture of Küng's more mature works, *On Being a Christian* and *Does God Exist?* [78] The German editions appeared respectively in the years 1974 and 1978. Küng succeeded in getting a wide hearing outside the Roman Catholic constituency. It was most unusual, certainly for Western Europe, that the voluminous and substantive study on the meaning of being a Christian became a bestseller. For thirty-seven weeks, it was on the top of the list in the secular illustrated German magazine, *Der Spiegel*.

Küng's major objective in these works was to highlight the relevance of Christian faith in today's complex society. Such a Christian stance required a functional rather than the traditional ontological Christology, according to Küng, which added fuel to the deepening conflict with Rome. Ever since the Christological debates in the early Church, a functional Christology had been frowned upon. For Küng, however, it is the Christ of history who addresses the human situation in a more concrete way than the definitions concerning the eternal logos.[79] The most controversial issue became Küng's use of terms like "advocate," "representative," or "delegate" for the function of Jesus' ministry. Again, an edition of essays by Catholic theologians was issued against Küng—this time against his functional Christology and its implications for exegesis and Christian life. Among the authors were Küng's former advisors, Hans Urs von Balthasar and Karl Rahner.[80] The response to his critics was incorporated in Küng's latest book on God's existence in life. Küng reiterated that he did not reject the classic formulations, but that functional terms bring Christ closer to modern man. Küng summarized: "For me, Jesus of Nazareth is the Son of God. For the whole significance . . . lies in the fact that in Jesus . . . the God who loves men is himself present and active." [81]

The years of zealous literary activity have caused lively discussion in Rome, in university halls, and, finally, in the media across the world. Küng began where Luther started, namely with the concept of justification by faith. For Luther, this meant separation from the Catholic Church, while, for Küng, it implied the hope for reunion of all Christians. As theological advisor, he stoutly promoted a new structure of the Church, and as religious antagonist during the seventies, Küng argued against the doctrine of the infallibility of the pope. During the years of increasing estrangement from the institutional Church, Küng began turning his attention to the needs of secular man. It is in this area where he wrote his most substantial works. The following chapters will analyze each crucial publication by Küng together with its attending circumstances. At the quincentennial celebration of the University of Tübingen, Küng affirmed: "It is the task of theology and subsequently of the Church's proclamation of the Gospel, too, to bring contemporary men and women, and scientists and scholars, into contact with God in such a way that this is not at the expense of people, or of their rationality or freedom or humanity." [82]

II

Justification by Faith

1. The Barthian Dialogue

The concept of "justification" may seem rather abstract to the contemporary reader. In the history of the Church, however, it has played a crucial role during times of theological conflict. Justification by God in Christ always indicated a soteriology of dependence on God rather than a reliance on personal initiative. In the days of the apostle Paul, for instance, this doctrine determined the absolute difference between Christian faith and the Jewish dependence on the obligations of the Law. For the Church Father Augustine, the doctrine of justification by grace was set forth in order to distinguish between faithful believers and Pelagianists relying on their free will. The Reformer, Martin Luther, discovered in this doctrine the decisive criterion for genuine protest against a Catholic emphasis on religious works. The contemporary theologian, Karl Barth, finally extended Luther's view by making justification by faith the normative distinction between an authentic Christian and anyone who does not completely and exclusively depend on Christ for his salvation. Barth rejected a humanistic dependence on reason as well as a pietist craving for experience. In either case, man's relationship to God is a result of personal achievement. For this reason, the doctrine of justification by grace became Barth's touchstone of theology.[1] It was, therefore, most natural that a Catholic theologian interested in dialogue would zoom in on this doctrine.

One of the first Catholic publications [2] on Karl Barth drew Küng's attention while he was studying in Rome.[3] It had been published in 1951 and was written by his compatriot, Hans Urs von Balthasar, chaplain at the University of Basel.[4] During a visit in von Balthasar's home, one of three themes mentioned to Küng concerned the doctrine of justification. During the following three years, Küng immersed himself in the history and meaning of this doctrine as interpreted by Barth as well as by Catholic authors and documents. In the process of formulating his text for two dissertations on the same subject, it gradually dawned upon Küng how crucial the doctrine of justification was for the dialogue between Catholics and Protestants.[5] He discovered how this doctrine stood in judgment upon Catholic practice and neglect. Barth's interpretations were "aimed not so much at individual doctrinal declarations as at the fundamental Catholic attitude. It is taken to be some kind of veiled unchristian humanism, a secret self-glorification of man. . . ." [6] Küng discovered also that the Council of Trent, organized to halt the Protestant movement, did not see the crucial implications of the doctrine of justification by grace. His greatest surprise was, however, that Barth's concept of justification could be reconciled with sources in early medieval Catholicism.[7] Küng did not hesitate to call Barth "one of the spiritual fathers of Catholic renewal." [8] At the same time he considered Barth to be more consistently Protestant than his pietist or Bultmannian coreligionists.

This theological concept enabled Barth and Küng to discover their common ground. Barth wrote in his introductory letter to Küng's controversial book on justification:

> The idea that I might be a crypto-Catholic or you a crypto-Protestant—let us hope that neither of these foolish notions will occur to any of your readers. Yet it is true, isn't it, that today a few on both sides, you and I among them, are coming to realize that, while we are divided in faith, we are divided within the same faith—the same, because and insofar as we and you can believe in the self-same Lord. Those who begin to see this may and must talk to one another, but with a new approach.[9]

Küng reflected the same excitement of discovery in his tribute to Karl Barth at his funeral in 1968:

> Sorrowing with you today are countless Catholics, theologians and laymen, everywhere on earth where the word of Karl Barth has encountered them in so many languages. . . . Our time urgently needs . . . the doctor of both theologies, Protestant and Catholic. And if anyone in our century has offered an outstanding example of this, it was Karl Barth.[10]

Through their encounter a common cause was presented to Catholics and Protestants alike. Küng's publication of 1957 contributed to the sudden breakthrough of the Second Vatican Council in 1962. During the intervening years, Barth and Küng were the spokesmen for an ecumenical encounter, both from a critical stance toward their own constituencies. Both have voiced their prophetic anger publicly: Barth before the opening assembly of the World Council of Churches, already in 1948, and Küng before the third session of Vatican II by his address on "Truthfulness in the Church." [11] Both men had strong convictions about the original and ultimate unity of God's Church; both were compulsive workers and have ostracized themselves by extreme statements; and both will be remembered as prophetic voices far outside their own constituencies. Characteristically for prophets, though, they were issue-oriented and, in many cases, little informed about the wider context of Christianity. Neither of these two theologians was much aware of evangelical Protestantism during and following the Reformation. The widespread movements of evangelism and missions during the nineteenth century was beyond the parameters of their intensive quest.

In spite of their common concerns, the differences between Barth and Küng were always there and gradually became more apparent. Initially their divergence was expressed in conviviality as the following anecdote illustrates.

> Many years ago we were discussing, as we did so often, the Pope and the Petrine office in the church. And as he did not then agree with me, I said smilingly: "Well, all right. I grant you good faith!" Thereupon he became serious and said: "So you allow me good faith. I have never conceded myself good faith. And when once the day comes when I have to appear before my Lord, then I will not come

with my deeds, with the volumes of my *Dogmatics* in the basket
upon my back. All the angels there would have to laugh. But then
I shall also not say, 'I have always meant well; I had good faith.'
No, then I will only say one thing: 'Lord, be merciful to me a poor
sinner!' " [12]

The tension between God's grace and man's faith, between a theocentric and an anthropocentric approach, remained typical throughout
the dialogue between Barth and Küng. Supposedly because of pastoral
concerns, Küng later chose consciously for a theology "from below"
in contrast to Barth's theology that presumed to be a theology "from
above." [13] Actually, though, this difference was a tension from the
very beginning. Around his fiftieth birthday, Küng mused: "Right
from the start this was a major point of difference between me and
Barth, who indeed rejected any true knowledge of God that was
not based on Christian revelation." [14] In his recent publication on
the existence of God, Küng, therefore, identified with Erikson's anthropocentric concept of "basic trust" being a psychological qualifica-
tion in the secular as well as in the religious realm.[15] Küng ultimately
wanted to be relevant to the contemporary scene, while Barth consistently attempted to formulate the normative Christian principle, whatever the implications.

Barth as well as Küng liked to use the illustration of the mirror
to indicate the dialectic complexity of the issues that must be seen
rather than analyzed. According to Küng, "The issue is not Barth
at all—and he would be the first to agree—but the confronting of
one another with the mirror of the gospel of Jesus Christ, in earnest
and uncompromising theological interchange." [16] Part of the complexity was that both Barth and Küng did not totally represent their
respective constituencies, that they did not agree completely with
one another, and that both were continually searching for new
formulations.[17] To shed some light upon their diatribe on the doctrine
of justification, this chapter will follow the classic components of
the doctrine in question.

2. By Grace Alone

"Why is it that all of Barth's other opponents [including people
of the most divergent orientations and even philosophers] stand a

better chance of being given a fair hearing and fair treatment than representatives of Catholic theology?" [18] Küng knows the answer to this question quite well as his own words in part one of his book indicate:

> This is why Barth reacts with such unusual sharpness to Catholic teaching, in an almost emotional way. This is why his questions are so full of irritation and so vehement—why his judgement is so hard, and at first glance, so one-sided and unjust: Barth sees the sovereign majesty of God's grace threatened. In the Catholic theology of justification . . . is not all emphasis primarily on man, on the creature? [19]

After having articulated Barth's doctrine of justification, Küng concludes with a brief chapter entitled "Open Questions." [20] These questions are to set the tone for his two hundred page response to Karl Barth. Actually, however, the questions as well as Küng's response are also directed to his Catholic readers. Among the many questions the following stand out: "Does the Catholic theology of justification take justification seriously as the sovereign act of God's grace?" "Do we not prefer to speak, and to speak almost exclusively, of man's state of grace, instead of God's acts of grace?" "Hasn't grace become something physical instead of being and remaining something personal?" "Do not all these questions taken together still amount to the manipulating of God, the managing of grace, the relativizing of the majesty and sovereignty of God?" "Is this not *the* crucial reason why the Reformers wanted to have nothing more to do with the Catholic Church?" "Is this not *the* reason why even today one cannot become Catholic?" The answer to all these rhetorical questions for Küng is, of course: "Yes, indeed!" Post-Reformation Catholic theology is off the track, according to Küng. It could regain its position of superiority if it would balance its enunciations with the convictions of pre-Tridentinian and pre-Thomistic theologians.

For Küng the first case of derailment in Catholic theology took place in opposition to the dogmatician, Peter Lombard (c. 1100–1160), who still spoke of an unmediated activity by the Holy Spirit in connection with salvation.[21] The concept of "created grace" or mediated grace was introduced a century later, in order to add to the direct activity of the Spirit the indirect or mediated grace bestowed upon the Church and upon its clergy and laity as a "treasure of grace." According to the medievalist, J. Auer, it was Albert the Great (c. 1200–1280), the teacher of Thomas Aquinas, who began emphasizing the mediated or created grace at the expense of the "uncreated grace" belonging to God alone.[22] In other words, the ecclesiastical institution as an agency of grace and man's experience took the place of God as the sole dispenser of grace. Barth reacted vehemently to the development of a series of distinctions between direct and indirect grace, between supernatural and natural grace, and even between the grace of God and the grace of Christ. "How dare we split up the grace of Christ and the grace of God in this way? . . . If there is *one* God, and *one* Mediator between God and man, and therefore *one* grace—what place is there for all these abstractions?"[23]

According to Küng, there *is* place for a distinction of the source and of the effect of grace as long as both receive equal emphasis. Küng concedes that according "to the New Testament the concept of 'grace' means first of all the favor and benevolence of God and of Christ, rarely the created inner quality of the soul."[24] Then there is also, however, John 14:23 that says: "We will come to him and make our home with him." The gifts of the Spirit, the "charisma's," also refer to a "graciousness" of man.[25] Taking all these aspects into consideration, Küng concludes that the medieval development of Catholic theology remained scriptural as long as balance and completeness were maintained. Grace never becomes at man's disposal, but he is possessed by it. Bonaventura's epigram is mentioned in this connection: "to hold is to be held,"[26] having grace is always a divine and alien reality, never man's own achievement, but it can take hold of him.

The fact of the matter is, though, that Luther was confronted by a post-Thomistic Church that presented itself as the sole dispenser of grace for the living as well as for the dead. Luther's protest against indulgence preachers who proclaimed that they could redeem a soul from purgatory was ignored in the debate with the Dominican friar, Johann Eck, in the summer of 1519.[27] There was, indeed, no basis for such teaching in the dogmas of the Catholic Church. The practice of selling indulgences was merely a matter of expedience. Since Luther could not be condemned for protesting against such practices, he was ultimately excommunicated as a heretic for his doctrine of justification by faith alone to the exclusion of grace bestowed by the Catholic Church, its sacraments, and its saints.[28]

Küng is quite correct when he reminds his readers "that it is the theology of justification that lies at the root of the still continuing theological battle over the true form of Christianity, at the root of the greatest catastrophe that has befallen the Catholic Church in her two-thousand-year history." [29] Barth concurred with Luther in the assertion that grace is granted by God alone. In the preface to his famous commentary on the book of Romans, Barth stated pointedly: "God is in Heaven, and thou art on earth." [30] As a consistent Protestant he felt compelled to reject any depository of grace given to the Church. According to Küng, both Barth and Luther overreacted to a Church that in spite of its imperfections is yet the body of Christ, the sacred mediatrix of grace. Grace "is not a private grace . . . it has an essentially ecclesiological character." [31]

As Luther protested against Thomism so Barth reacted to the formulations of the Council of Trent that convened over a period of almost twenty years (1545–63) to formulate a defense against the Reformation. Since the Reformers wanted to return to an unmediated grace of God, the Tridentine fathers had to underline the mediated grace or the "habitus" of man. In their defense Küng stated: "The Reformers actually provoked a certain anthropocentricity in the decree on justification through their own deficient interpretation of Christian revelation." [32] Küng even accused the Protestants of neglect! "The limits of Trent might have been less noticeable had the theologians from northern Europe, and especially the Protestants, accepted the invitation and appeared in Trent." [33] Küng also noted that conciliar decrees are by nature one-sided because "the majority of dogmatic definitions are *polemic formulations* pronounced against heresies." [34]

Whatever the circumstances may have been, Barth accepted no excuse and reacted most vehemently to the decree listed in Denzinger 797 that stated: "It (the Synod) furthermore declares . . . that justification must be derived from the predisposing grace . . . so that they who by sin were turned away from God, through His stimulating and assisting grace are disposed to convert themselves to their own justification, by freely assenting to and cooperating with the same grace. . . ." [35] The stumbling block for Karl Barth was, of course, the term "cooperating." Küng retorted that Barth misunderstood

the Latin sense of this term. No collaboration was meant, but rather
a form of participation or involvement in the process of justification.[36]
Again, Küng resorted to early medieval theology for support of his
position. In this case, he quoted Bernard of Clairvaux from his discussion on grace and the free will, where Clairvaux stated: "It is by
God therefore without doubt that the beginning of our salvation is
made, not through us at all nor with our cooperation. Yet consent
and the work, though they are not of us, are now not without us." [37]
Barth could have responded that Clairvaux at least rejected the term
"cooperation" in arguing for an element of "consent."

Below, in the discussion of the section "By Faith Alone," it will
be demonstrated that Barth retracted his absolute position on grace.[38]
Evangelicals, though, would rather maintain firmly the "unmediated"
grace of the early Middle Ages and consider the later developments
of Thomism and Trent as forms of deterioration. Luther's affirmation
of grace alone has found its way into the hymn authored by John
Newton: "Amazing grace! how sweet the sound, that saved a wretch
like me." Evangelical Protestants would not consider it a lack of
theological refinement that no credit is given to the sinner for his
consent or participation. They feel part of the Puritan tradition that
has no place for any merit of man. As Isaac Watts expressed it so
eloquently: "Forbid it, Lord, that I should boast, save in the death
of Christ my God." Unmediated grace has remained the Evangelical
Protestant conviction of a direct access to God.

3. By Scripture Alone

The doctrine of grace focused upon God as the source of salvation.
On this point Catholic theology and Protestantism are in agreement.
It was Thomistic theology with its emphasis on "created grace" that
gave rise to the deplorable conflict of the Reformation. The medieval
scholastics had extolled the ecclesiastic grace to a treasure that was
to be dispensed to the faithful by means of the "channels of grace."
These channels were foremost the seven sacraments by which the
believers were to be saved and sanctified.[39] Luther, however, attributed justification and sanctification to the Word alone. Not only
were the sacraments reduced to two—baptism and the Lord's Supper—[40] but also the sacraments themselves were depreciated to mere
visible expressions of the Word.[41] The unmediated Word of God

was associated with the "mighty fortress" of God extolled in Psalm 46. One of the stanzas of the Reformation hymn reminds one graphically of this Protestant principle:

> That word above all earthly pow'rs,
> No thanks to them, abideth.

As was stated above in connection with the doctrine of grace, Küng is in basic agreement with Catholic theology in his affirmation of the ecclesiological character of grace.[42] "The grace of God in Jesus Christ has been given us through the Holy Spirit in the Church." [43] Küng observed with satisfaction that the Lutheran World Federation has come to an agreement with the Catholic hierarchy on the doctrine of justification. Their discussion was held in 1971 on the isle of Malta. Their report read: "Lutherans and Catholics are agreed that the Gospel is the foundation of Christian freedom . . . But since Christian freedom is linked with witness to the Gospel, it requires institutional forms for its mediation." [44]

Küng does not call attention to the difference between Luther and contemporary Lutherans. The linkage between the Word and the institution was a major obstacle for Luther. The Word of God may, indeed, use many ways and methods, but it is not tied to institutional channels, according to authoritative interpreters of Luther.[45] Other Protestants stayed closer to the unmediated character of the Word. Calvin spoke of special illumination as God's interpretative agent, while the Baptists claimed the "soul competency" of the believer in understanding the word of salvation. All evangelical Protestants agree in not accepting any authoritative institutional medium in their interpretation of the Scriptures.

The controversial term for the early Lutherans and the Council of Trent was the concept "Tradition of Faith." Trent advocated the Church as the sole authoritative interpreter of the Scriptures. This interpretation has been preserved in its sacred tradition. As the Fathers of Trent stated: "The purity itself of the Gospel is preserved in the Church . . . this truth and instruction are contained in the written books and in the unwritten traditions . . . which are held in veneration with an equal affection of piety and reverence . . . since one God is the author of both . . ." [46]

At first glance, Küng seems to agree with the Reformers rather than with the Fathers of Trent in his value judgment of tradition. Küng stated explicitly: "The Word of God, in the *strictest* sense, is *Sacred Scripture* alone." Küng argued that the terms "equal affection of piety and reverence" used by Trent for both Scripture and tradition as sources of revelation do not imply that tradition is inspired in the same sense as Sacred Scripture. Both Scripture and tradition are, indeed, manifestations of the same source. In order to distinguish between their functions, Küng suggested that the Scripture "*is* the unmediated Word of God . . . , while the documents of tradition only *contain* the Word of God." [47] Küng concluded: "The Catholic theologian feels bound at this point not only in a relative but in an absolute way" to tradition.[48]

Küng not only identified himself consciously with the Catholic concepts of Scripture and tradition, he also discovered in Barth an affinity for a duality of revelation. This is possible because Barth started out from the transcendent nature of the Word of God. Its immanent manifestations are the Word incarnate, the Word written, and the Word proclaimed.[49] God's Word is dialectically involved in the human word. Next to Christ and the Scriptures is the living word of proclamation, which is projected into creeds, theology, and confessions. Such a position is, indeed, close to Küng's view when he stated: "The Scripture has been the *first* font of Catholic dogmatic theology . . . free of error, valid for all times and places, and most important of all, inexhaustible." [50] The Scripture, however, has to be read and interpreted within the context of the Church. As such the Scripture is therefore incomplete rather than insufficient for the individual believer, according to Küng.[51]

From a philosophical perspective, Küng finds more affinity with Barth than with his conservative Catholic colleagues. Küng rejected their scholastic division between faith and reason and cherished Barth's dialectic unity of all knowledge. Küng warned his readers and stated:

> Catholic theologians will have no small difficulty in trying to grasp the theology of Karl Barth, and this precisely because, quite apart from all matters of context, Barth thinks and speaks otherwise than they do. The vocabulary and the whole system of categories, the choice of words and the pattern of thinking are strange. Whereas the Catholic theologian generally thinks and speaks along Aristotelian

and scholastic lines, Barth's thought and language take their shape from German Idealism.[52]

Already the French Catholic theologian, Father Henri de Lubac, had criticized the Aristotelian approach in Catholic dogma. Hans Urs von Balthasar had joined the "Nouvelle Théologie" and, consequently, had resigned from the Jesuit order for the same reason.[53] Although Küng also adopted an antischolastic attitude, he did not feel estranged from the Catholic Church and its official theology. Küng did refer in his later works contemptuously to its "Stockwerk Theorie" in English, the "two-tier theory," namely a reasoning in the two levels of nature and supernature, or of faith and reason.[54] According to Barth and Küng, the Word of God is one dialectic unity of transcendent and immanent quality like the incarnation of Christ unites both the divine and human natures. In reference to the Scriptures, this position means that the Word of God equally transcends as pervades the textual document. Küng even felt compelled to call this the philosophy of the Scripture, as he stated: "One can perhaps approach Barth's thought processes most readily from Sacred Scripture." [55]

One may summarize that Küng discovered agreement between Barth and Roman Catholicism in a theological sense. Their difference may be in philosophical thought patterns, but some Catholic pioneers, Küng included, already challenged the more traditional Catholic theologians to revamp their philosophy. This is the line of argument not only in Küng's first publication but in all his later publications as well. For this reason, Küng cannot accord Luther full praise for his heroic reform, because theologically he saw no real difference between Rome and Reformation. For Küng there was only a historical basis for Luther's disagreement with Rome. There were, indeed, abuses, but those were not the result of a theological position. On this point, Küng followed the monastic leader, Father Yves Congar, who already before World War I had pointed out that merely nontheological factors were the cause of the Reformation. Congar saw it as a conflict between the impetuous prophet Luther and the more conservative institutional representatives of Rome.[56]

Küng more concretely attributed the Reformation to Luther's intractable subjectivism as he observed in his next book on *The Council, Reform and Reunion:* "Luther set his personal, subjective, and yet [by his intention] universally binding interpretation of the Scriptures *in principle* above the Church and her tradition." [57] The question remains, however: Is Luther's motto "By Scripture alone" a mere expression of "psychological and religious sentiment" [58] leading to a "bedevilled situation" [59] or is here an authentic theological principle involved? Evangelical Protestants, more than four hundred and fifty years later and in a totally different sociological context, still cling to the sole authority of the Scriptures. They still subject all later interpretation to a critical analysis. Unawarely, tradition may develop but it never can claim authority, not even in a derived sense.

4. By Faith Alone

The doctrine of justification points to God's grace as the source of salvation, to the Scriptures as its medium, and to faith as the response of man. Luther's earliest discovery of man's faith as the only condition of salvation was during the "Tower Experience" in 1513. In preparing his lecture on Romans 1:17 for the succeeding day, Luther discovered a new dimension. "He who through faith is righteous shall live." Luther called these words later "the very gate of paradise." [60] The gospel of a gracious rather than of a stern and judgmental God is received in grateful acceptance. Man is saved by responding in faith rather than by works of morality, of devotions, of indulgences, or by penitential castigations. When Luther, a few years later, translated the New Testament, he felt free to add the word "alone" to the text in Romans 3:28: "For we hold that a man is justified by faith *alone* apart from works of law." This was not a real innovation either! Küng referred in this connection to a German translation of 1483 where the affirmation "by faith alone" already occurred.[61]

Barth has a forceful excursus in his *Church Dogmatics* on the Tridentine teaching concerning the relation of faith and works. He focused on the notorious canon 9 of session VI.

> If anyone shall say that by faith alone the sinner is justified, so as to understand that nothing else is required to cooperate in the attainment of the grace of justification, and that it is in no way necessary that he be prepared and disposed by the action of his own will: let him be anathema.[62]

Catholic scholars, Küng included, argue that the reference "by faith alone" ought to be interpreted in the light of canon 12 that stated:

> If anyone shall say that justifying faith is nothing else than confidence in the divine mercy which remits sins for Christ's sake, or that it is this confidence alone by which we are justified: let him be anathema.[63]

Although Barth can concur with canon 12 in the rejection of a mere experiential faith, he does not agree that this canon is a commentary on canon 9. Justification by faith was for Luther not just an experience of confidence, but rather an act of total surrender. Barth assumed that the Tridentine Fathers would have known this. After reading Küng's reinterpretation, Barth was willing to express his admiration for Küng's argument. He did not concede, however, any misrepresentation by himself, but rather pleaded for mitigating circumstances in his supposed lack of understanding of the Tridentine text, and then continued his defense in the following manner:

> How do you explain the fact that all this could remain hidden so long, and from so many, both outside and inside the Church? And now for my own salvation, may I just whisper a question (a very confidential question, but one not liable to detract from your book in the mind of any serious reader): Did you yourself discover all this before you so carefully read my *Church Dogmatics* or was it while you were reading it afterward? [64]

Thus, Barth as well as Küng sees a possibility of the meeting of the minds. The articles of Trent can be explained and complemented in such a manner that they would satisfy Barth. Küng does assert, however, that "the Reformers actually provoked a certain anthropocentricity in the decree on justification through their own deficient interpretation of Christian revelation." [65] After four hundred years of isolated existence, one should be able to bring together the minds separated because of mutual repercussions.

Both Barth and Küng redefine the exclusive concept "by faith alone" in claiming that faith includes elements of love, hope, and fear. Barth supported his view by referring to Luther's description of faith as "a living, active, busy thing." [66] Küng referred to Catholic dogma that states that "man through Jesus Christ . . . receives . . . all these gifts at the same time: faith, hope, and charity." [67] Both Barth and Küng are of the opinion that justification as well as sanctification are only different moments of God's total act toward man. Küng observed that Protestant tradition has generally considered sanctification as an act of response by man occurring after the experience of salvation, while Catholic tradition has primarily understood sanctification to be the ontological aspect of faith achieved by God.[68] A brief survey of Scripture passages, though, supports the Protestant viewpoint. In quoting Romans 6:19, Küng has simply to concede that Paul exhorts his readers to "yield their members to righteousness for sanctification after they have been justified." [69]

The Catholic scholar, Moeller, gave credit to Calvin for having introduced a clear distinction between justification and sanctification.[70] At this point, though, Barth parted with the Calvinist view and followed the Catholic tradition by saying: Sanctification is not . . . "a second divine action which either takes place simultaneously with it, or precedes or follows it in time. The action of God . . . is unitary." [71] Justification and sanctification are connected as reconciliation and conversion or as forgiveness and new life. This new life is even called by the controversial term of "good works." These are not good because they are an active response of man, but rather "because they are praised by God and done to His praise." [72] Barth as well as Küng, then, asserts an inclusive faith, which for the former means a total engagement of man and for the latter means a claim for a religion of penitent response.

In this connection, Küng has to discuss one more obscure text in the canon of Trent dealing with the recompense of the saved. The most controversial passage on merits is in Denzinger 809 reading as follows: "And therefore to those who work well 'unto the end' [Matthew 10:22], and who trust in God, life eternal is to be proposed, both as a grace mercifully promised . . . and as a recompense . . . faithfully given to their good works and merits." Küng claims that a distinction should be made between reward and merit, which the Council of Trent only brings out implicitly. Supported by *Kittel's Theological Dictionary*, Küng described reward as an eschatological reality based upon man's total religious attitude, while the Pharisaic notion of moral merit is rejected throughout the New Testament.[73] According to Küng, the Council of Trent spoke about the eschatologic reward even though the term "merit" was used. The statement just quoted is addressed "to those who work well 'unto the end' " and to those "who trust in God." Küng summarized his apology with a quote from Denzinger: "Nevertheless, a Christian should have no inclination either to rely on himself or to glory in himself instead of the Lord [2 Cor. 10:17], whose goodness towards all men is such that he wants his gifts to be their merits." [74]

The Catholic scholar, Otto Karrer, conceded that the concept of merit is a questionable commodity produced by the religious "industry." Even though Protestants have their dubious methods and terms, too, Karrer warned his Catholic readers "that such pedagogical deficiencies do not go uncorrected—partly thanks to the Protestant 'thorn.' " [75]

The clarion call of the Reformation has been muffled by theological qualifications that gradually dissolved the power of the adjective "alone" in the affirmations "by grace alone," "by Scripture alone," and "by faith alone." Hans Küng has traced this tendency in Karl Barth. The maxim "by grace alone," for Karl Barth, has to be inclusive of the Church and its functions of worship and proclamation, because "the appropriation of the grace of Christ donated to us occurs for the individual *only within the community.*" [76] The concept "by Scripture alone" had to shed its uniqueness for the benefit of the absolute Word of God that transcends its avenues of the Word incarnate, the Word written, and the Word proclaimed. Finally, Küng's diatribe with Barth brought to light that also in the affirmation "by faith alone," the adjective "alone" is weakened by making faith inclusive of sanctification. Küng has rendered theology invaluable service by his analysis; nonetheless, he should have been aware that Barth does not represent all Protestants, certainly not American Evangelicalism. Its protest has emphatically been expressed against Barth's definition of the Scriptures. The Evangelicals have preserved also a low view of the Church and its ordinances, so that they still can affirm with Luther a salvation by grace *alone* presented to man through the Scriptures *alone* aiming for a response by faith *alone*.

5. By Christ Alone

As was demonstrated above, both Barth and Küng deem personal faith to exist only within the context of the divinely instituted religion.

This is why grace cannot be presented without the superstructure
or substructure of the Church. To claim a foundation for this universal
Church as the realm of salvation, the doctrine of Christ as the logos
of creation becomes essential. Küng asserted, therefore: "Justification
is not the central dogma of Christianity. . . . The central *dogma*
of *Christ*ianity is the mystery of *Christ* . . . the mystery of the
total creation. . . . Christian theology is the theology of
revelation." [77] Küng demonstrated that Barth, too, focused on the
creative role of Christ in order to underscore the universal validity
of Christian revelation. Küng's quest for Catholicity met Barth's
search for a normative absolute. Barth declared unambiguously: "In
Jesus Christ we are not merely dealing with the author of our justification and sanctification. . . . But at the same time and beyond, all
that . . . He is the 'first-born of all creation' [Col. 1:16]—the *first*
and *eternal* Word of God delivered and fulfilled in time." [78] In
support for his position, it is not difficult for Küng to quote a good
selection of Pauline and Johannine passages on the preexistent and
creative role of Christ.[79] For both Küng and Barth, salvation history
is the manifestation of the eternal truth of God in Jesus Christ.
The doctrine of justification should, therefore, be anchored solidly
in the doctrine of creation.

There is another agreement in Barth and Küng, namely that both
observe a certain superficiality in their respective constituencies; they
point to a general neglect of the logos concept in favor of mere
soteriological concerns. According to Küng, modern Catholic theology
has perpetuated the Thomistic separation of nature and grace and
is thereby losing its universal claim involving nature as well as
grace.[80] As in the discussion of the concept of grace, Küng again
resorted to Bernard of Clairvaux for a reformulation of genuine Catholic theology. Bernard and other medieval mystical authors restored
the biblical and early Christian insights in the unique role of Christ
in the work of creation.[81] Christ is not to be contrasted with a "Cre-
ator-God" as was asserted in the various forms of Gnosticism.[82]
Salvation should be grounded in God's creation rather than be isolated from it. Küng summarized the teaching of the Greek Fathers
in the following manner: "He through whom we had already been
created has to come to re-create us." [83]

There is a shade of difference, however, between Barth's universal
validity of revelation and Küng's ontological Catholicity in Christ.
Barth averred that in Jesus Christ the family of man is elected,

which means that Christ is "the electing God" as well as "the elected man." [84] This gracious and at the same time righteous election is the eternal agreement or covenant with mankind. For this reason, every human being is by very existence entirely under the grace and judgment of God. God allows man to live for His glory and provides for each individual the decisive options for eternal salvation or condemnation.

Does this mean that history is a deterministic dramatization of an "eternal decree," as Calvin called it? Not at all! Küng quoted Barth's response: "In the course of God's eternal deciding we have constantly to reckon with new decisions in time. As the Bible itself presents the matter, there is no election which cannot be followed by rejection, no rejection which cannot be followed by election." [85] Therefore, man's sin is a real breaking of the covenant that necessitates a genuine reconciliation through Christ, who had to take humanity's place so that He became their advocate. In characteristic fashion Barth stated: "It was the *Judge* who was judged, who let Himself be judged. Because He was a *man* like us. He was able to be judged like us." [86]

The eternal decision of God became for Barth manifest in the cross and resurrection of Jesus Christ. Küng, however, talked about the eternal being of God revealed in the incarnation of Christ.[87] The difference between Barth's redemptive approach and Küng's incarnational approach is not only typical of their denominational background, but allows also for other differences. The redemptive action of God in Christ provides a challenge to individuals to either give adherence to Christ or to reject him.[88] Küng, however, in following the Catholic tradition, speculated about the mystery of Christ present in the Church. "Thus it comes as no surprise that it is precisely the mystery of the *Church*—or the mystery of Christ—that is hidden in *creation.*" [89] The contrast between his organic ecclesiological view and Barth's personal soteriology may not be essential to Küng,[90] for Evangelical Protestants it was, and still is, of utmost importance. Personal salvation is considered an individual encounter with Christ resulting in redemption from sin and rebirth into a new life. The "whosoever" of John 3:16 is quoted emphatically by Evangelicals of various stripes. At this point, even Barth who allowed for a degree of organic unity in the elected Christ, kept firmly to an individual encounter with the Savior.

Whether redemptively personal or incarnationally ecclesiastic,

Barth, as well as Küng, believed in an effective justification, an act of God in Christ that achieves what it proclaims. Both argued strongly against a merely forensic or juridical conception of justification; both accepted God's word as a creative agency.[91] Küng signaled at this point Barth's divergence from the Reformation; [92] but Barth himself affirmed his diverging position clearly and with conviction: "[Justification] is a declaring righteous which without any reserve can be called a *making* righteous." [93]

Evangelical Protestant theologians, however, have been keen to stress the declarative righteousness of a Christian in distinction from an effective righteousness. Luther's principle of the "simul justus, simul peccator" [94] also underscored the dual existence of being declared holy and of being actually sinful at the same time. Luther wanted to protect himself against an indirect salvation by works, whereby the ultimate results of salvation would allow God proleptically to declare a sinner just. Again, Evangelical hymns confirm this tradition. Isaac Watts sang about the cross "on which the Prince of Glory died," while Fanny J. Crosby would pray, "Jesus keep me near the cross." The experience of salvation is redemption while the effect of a life in sanctification is not mentioned in the same breath.

The crown witness for Küng is the Anglican theologian, J. Henry Newman, who became cardinal after his conversion to Roman Catholicism. It was his contention that the doctrine of forensic justification was the cause for hypocrisy and noninvolvement among his constituency.[95] Newman, therefore, devoted considerable time to reformulate the doctrine of justification, which study was in turn a factor for his transition to Catholicism. In his *Lectures of Justification* (1838), Newman asserted: "First, that justification is, in the proper meaning of the word, a *declaration* of righteousness; secondly, that it is distinct from renewal; thirdly, that it is the *antecedent* or *efficient cause* of renewal." [96]

Like Newman, Küng drew his biblical argument from the Word of creation. "God said, 'Let there be light' and there was light. Jesus said: 'Be clean' and it was clean . . . He says: 'This is My body' and it is His body." [97] From this quote, it is obvious that the interpretation of the doctrine of effective justification is related to sacramentalism in general. The facts that Newman became Catholic and that Barth and Küng agreed on the effectiveness of the Word places them in a camp other than the Evangelical Free Churches. Believing in forensic justification demands only God's Word of forgiveness through Christ. Consequentially, most Free Churches do not accept sacramental channels of grace, but rather believe in divine ordinances such as baptism and the Lord's Supper.

Even though Küng and Barth may agree on the unity of forensic and effective justification, their conservative constituencies are still far apart on this issue, which is reflected in their worship and devotion. Küng went through multiple sets of categories polarizing orthodox Protestants and traditional Catholics. While the former confessed an objective juridical concept of justification, the latter holds to a subjective mystical experience of salvation. Likewise, the orthodox categories of extrinsic and imputational justification are countered by intrinsic and communal experience of traditional Catholic devotion.[98] Küng challenged mature Catholics and Protestants to discover that both aspects of justification are equally essential, the declarative as well as the effective.

Küng concluded, when Protestants speak "of a declaring just which includes a making just; and Catholics of a making just which supposes a declaring just. Is it not time to stop arguing about imaginary differences?" [99] It certainly would be high time if, indeed, these differences were merely imaginary. Rather than considering Newman or Barth as representative cases for Protestantism, Küng should have included in his analysis the 465 years of post-Reformation history. Western Christianity has undergone major morphological changes since the Reformation. If the doctrine of justification is at the root of this centrifugal force, as Küng maintained it is,[100] then its interpretation cannot be of merely imaginary implications. The Reformation has created new forms of society; it has spawned daring scientific ventures and has created new economic and political systems. The sense of being declared righteous apparently had a major impact upon Christian initiative and therefore cannot be called imaginary.

6. Assessment

The publication on the doctrine of justification, Küng's first introduction to the general public, drew reaction from all sides. Neither the Protestants nor the Catholics could accept or believe that the Reformation was merely an incident in the process of history caused by unfortunate psychological or sociological circumstances. No one could believe that all the hard theological work had been merely a juggling with words. As was mentioned in chapter 1, the curia set up a file for the case Küng,[101] but it did not find adequate reason to discipline its prophetic apostle. Protestant scholars reluctantly accepted Küng's illustrious publication mainly because Karl Barth had endorsed this book as an authentic presentation of his views. In testimonial language Barth stated: "I here gladly, gratefully, and publicly testify . . . that you have adequately covered all significant aspects of justification treated in the ten volumes of my *Church Dogmatics* published so far. . . ." [102] Before anyone could devote an intensive analysis of the issue presented, Vatican II demanded all attention. The issue of justification was lost in the plethora of publications by Küng and other Catholic theologians followed during the sixties raising a wide range of issues.

In this chapter, only a few conclusions can be drawn. First of all, Küng has rendered a significant service by carefully analyzing the crucial theological issue between Protestantism and Catholicism. No attempt at mutual understanding had been made over a period of four and a half centuries. It was a painstaking effort to crystallize the lines of thought from the maze of similar terminology with different meanings. Küng has demonstrated that Barth, in spite of his anti-Romanism, was basically oriented toward a Catholic position. In almost every aspect of the doctrine of justification, Barth had a similar concern as the Council of Trent. Barth wanted to remove the sharp edges from the Reformation motto: "by faith alone, by Scripture alone, and by Christ alone." The Council of Trent went further and added a balancing element to each; for the Tridentine Fathers, they became faith *and* works, Scripture *and* tradition, Christ *and* the Church. Küng has succeeded to do justice to the Council as well as to Barth. He has reminded Catholics as well as Protestants of their unfinished business. From this perspective, it is regrettable that Küng did not include the Evangelical Protestant position in his discussion. It would have prevented the generalization that Barth is the representative of all Protestants, and Küng would have to acknowledge that the issues surrounding the doctrine of justification have not been resolved yet.

III
Renewal and Reunion

1. Defining the Task

One of the surprising turns of Roman Catholic history during this century was the election of Cardinal Angelo Giuseppe Roncalli, patriarch of Venice, to succeed Pope Pius XII. On 4 November 1958, Roncalli was solemnly inducted and crowned as Pope John XXIII. The vote for the relatively unknown patriarch came as a complete surprise to the seventy-six-year-old candidate himself as well as to the leaders of the Church at large. The impression was given that the cardinals in Rome wanted an interim pope after the strong centralist leadership of the angelic Pope Pius XII. No time for respite was forthcoming, however. During his four and a half years in office, more incisive changes took place than under any pope with longer service. Already his assumed name, John XXIII, could have raised suspicions. Had there not been a deposed pope by that name convening the controversial Council of Constance in 1415? Was it wise to remind Catholics and Protestants of that dark page in Church history? Was not the illicit execution of the precursor of the Reformation, John Huss, an embarassing issue for the Catholics and a stumbling block for the Protestants ever since Luther? [1]

The new pope adopted knowingly his name as well as his motto:

"obedience and peace" that turned out to be an attitude of obedience
to a servant Church and a search for peace with the Protestants
and the secular world. Too long the Roman Catholic community
had ignored the issues of the Reformation and too slavishly it had
isolated itself from the modern scientific and cultural developments.[2]
The newly elected Holy Father coined the phrase "aggiornamento,"
which indicated that the Church had to "adapt" itself to the modern
world. It is told that the little peasantlike pope had graphically demonstrated his intentions to a visitor by opening a window and allowing
a breath of fresh air to enter the stuffy hallways of the Vatican
palace.

This surprising turn of events was also significant for Dr. Hans
Küng. The year 1958 had been for him a period of wind stillness
before the storm. As assistant pastor in Lucerne, he had been introducing reforms in religious instruction and even in worship and
parish organization. Even though he felt a vocation to the pastorate,
Küng had already committed himself to a teaching career during
the fall of the preceding year.[3] He had received an invitation to a
scholarly lecture by Karl Barth. Exactly six days before the dramatic
announcement by Pope John XXIII concerning an ecumenical council,[4] Küng delivered his address at the University of Basel on 19
January 1959. He had chosen to speak on a Calvinist theme appropriate for the crucial era of change in the Catholic Church. In his
later writings and lectures, Küng would often refer to this theme
by the Latin phrase: "Ecclesia semper reformanda," [5] the Church
needs continuing reform.

Both Küng and Pope John XXIII had been decisively influenced
by Father Yves Congar,[6] the dedicated French Dominican theologian
who courageously championed the cause of ecumenism long before
the triumphalist era of Pope Pius XII. Already during World War
I, Congar had experienced the hospitality of French Protestants and,
in later years, he was deeply impressed by the annual weeks of
prayer for Christian unity promoted by Abbot Couturier.[7] He, of
course, had followed with great interest the development of the ecumenical movement in the non-Catholic churches. Congar's first book
on the subject of *Divided Christendom* was published in 1937 [8] and
his most controversial book on "True and False Reform" appeared
in 1950.[9] It was for Congar a time of "denunciations, warnings,
restrictive or discriminatory measures and mistrustful interventions"

by the hierarchy.[10] His plans for reforms, however, concerned mainly an inner revitalization of the Church along the same lines as Pope John XXIII proclaimed later by his "aggiornamento." Congar wrote in 1937: "I believe more than ever that the essential ecumenical activity of the Catholic Church should be to live its own life more fully and genuinely." [11] The election of Pope John XXIII was a genuine fulfillment of the aspirations of Father Congar. The creative pope projected Congar's ideas on the wide screen of the world community and opened the Council with a "Message to Humanity." It closed with the challenge: "We humbly and ardently call for all men to work along with us in building up a more just and brotherly city in this world. . . . Our prayer is . . . there may radiate the light of our great hope in Jesus Christ, our only Savior." [12]

Küng's focus of concern was, however, more narrow than the worldwide vision of Pope John XXIII. Küng limited his efforts to the theological breach between Rome and Luther. He gave little or no attention to the Orthodox Churches, the Calvinists, the Anglicans, or the Anabaptists. Like Congar, the young Swiss theologian saw in Luther the culprit of the schismatic reform movement, but unlike Congar, Küng considered the conflict increasingly a theological issue. In his defamed book on true and false reform, Congar had pleaded for a reform of life in the Church rather than yielding to the false attempts of reformulating doctrine. Küng, however, expected a more academic discussion. His second book was written in the year 1959 while he served as an academic assistant at the University of Münster that had a Roman Catholic faculty as well as a Protestant one. Interconfessional dialogue came easy and Küng was greatly impressed by its potential for renewed relationships. Within a year he had formulated his ideas about *The Council, Reform and Reunion.*

The American edition of this publication was more provocative than the German edition, which had carefully avoided the term "reform" in its title as well as in its content.[13] Congar and Barth had suggested to speak of "renewal" rather than of "reform." Even though Congar had devoted an extensive section in his book on true and false reform on the use of the term "reform" in the Scriptures as well as in the early and late Middle Ages,[14] he was well aware that the concept "reform" would evoke associations with the Protestant Reformation. Conservative Roman Catholic Church leaders might misunderstand the suggestion to reform as an undermining of the

divine and infallible institution of the Roman Catholic Church. Küng
conceded that the concepts "Reformer" and "Reformed Churches"
were among Calvin's favorite words. According to Küng, however,
there is need for reform as long as it is a form of "renewal" or
"adaptation" to modern situations. He reminded his readers of the
meaning of the term "aggiornamento," which he translated as a
"bringing-up-to-the-present-day." Küng rejected reform as "revolution," in the sense of a radical overthrow of institutions, while he
also repudiated reform as "restoration," being simply a resurrection
of old traditions and regulations.[15]

To create an optimum of goodwill, Küng decided to follow the
advice of his "fatherly friend," Karl Barth. Consequently, the German
title became: "The Council and Reunion: Renewal as a Summons
to Unity." [16] An ecumenical dialogue at Harvard University in 1963
demonstrated how relevant the issue of reform was also among American theologians. Martin A. Schmidt proved from historical records
that even Luther used the word "reformatio" reluctantly.[17] As a
rule, Protestant as well as Catholic theologians have always argued
for renewal rather than for innovation; they have aimed for a revival
of models or texts from the past rather than for dreams of a utopian
future. No wonder that Küng's first publication in the English language created shock and admiration. Henry P. Van Dusen admired
the combination of "fearless fidelity to truth and genuine piety" [18]
while others criticized him vehemently as being naive and eccentric.[19]
His first lecture tour in the United States during the spring of 1963
created the same ambivalent response; the University of St. Louis
awarded Küng an honorary LL.D. while the Catholic University of
America in Washington, D.C. banned him from lecturing.

2. Renewal through Dialogue

"We do not wish to put anyone in history on trial; we shall not
seek to establish who was right and who was wrong. Responsibility
is divided. We only want to say: Let us come together, let us make
an end of our divisions." [20] These words by Pope John XXIII spoken
during the first months of his ministry expressed a pragmatic intention
for reconciliation among all Christians. Congar as well as Küng would
have wanted a statement of confession for the corporate guilt of
Catholics as well as of Protestants for the tragic division in European

and Western Christianity. Hans Küng expressed his aspirations in his book on the Council.

> It would be a truly Christian act if the Pope and the Council . . . were to express this truth: Forgive us our sins! Forgive us our sins, and in particular our share in the sin of schism! Pope Adrian VI said it, long ago. An honest, humble confession of this sort by the leaders of the Church today would be pleasing to our heavenly Father as few words or deeds could be; and one word of repentance would open more doors to us among our separated fellow Christians than any number of pressing invitations to return.[21]

Pope Paul VI, the successor of John XXIII, did indeed open the second session of Vatican II with a sentence of conditional repentance. "If we are in any way to blame for that separation, we humbly beg God's forgiveness." This pope offered also his willingness to forgive and forget "the grief endured during the long series of dissensions and separations." [22]

A mere pragmatic forgetting of past offenses provides, however, no solid ground for reconciliation. Küng was correct when he wanted to reevaluate history and theology to create a basis of mutual acceptance. As long as Luther is considered a revolutionary, a criminal, a psychopath, or simply a heretic, no appreciation of his followers can be expected for people harboring such opinions.[23] Providentially great work had been done by the Catholic historian and professor, Josef Lortz. His epochal two-volume study on the Reformation in Germany appeared on the eve of World War II.[24] For the first time since the Reformation a sympathetic interpretation of Luther was presented by a Roman Catholic scholar. The hero of Wittenberg "was a great and fervent believer, filled with the faith that moves mountains. He burned with love for the Lord Jesus and his zeal for preaching the Gospel was unquenchable." [25] The author's conclusion is strangely disappointing, however. He averred that Luther's strong faith led him to a subjective ecclecticism focusing on God's grace and man's total depravity. Consequently, Lutheranism lost itself in rationalism and pietism, while "today the Catholic Church may justly claim to have taken care of concerns important to the Reformers better than they have done themselves." [26]

Even though this conclusion implies still a prejudiced value judg-

ment, it had come a long way since the first Catholic Luther interpreter, John Cochlaus, who had depicted Luther simply as one who
"lusted after wine and women." [27] Hans Küng readily follows Lortz
by referring to Luther's one-sided stress on certain articles of faith
that made him vulnerable to misunderstanding of other doctrines
that actually caused him to be heretical at certain points. A whole
"bedevilled situation" supposedly resulted from Luther's psychological and religious temperament.[28]

In the same breath, Küng mentioned fortunately also a more conscious and theological reason for the conflict between Luther and
Rome. "He brought the very essence of the Catholic Church into
question when (this was the real innovation) he set his personal,
subjective, and yet (by his intention) universally binding interpretation of the Scriptures *in principle* above the Church and her
tradition." [29] Küng's implied verdict is that Luther with such an
attitude excommunicated himself. By contrast, Küng mentioned the
example of St. Francis who remained within the Catholic community
of faith in spite of similar concerns for reform. Küng also mentioned
Bernard of Clairvaux who rebuked the pope in public, and Dante
who placed three popes in hell by his literature, yet, they and others
remained faithful to the papacy, while Luther "cared nothing for
the Church's excommunication." [30] Since later history evidenced continuing divisiveness following Luther's act of protest, Küng concluded
his scant historical assessment with a justification of the Roman
Catholic authorities of Luther's day.

Some clarification is needed concerning Küng's understanding of
the concept of "dialogue." This term shares a similar ambivalence
with the concept of "ecumenical" as used by Catholic leaders. Even
the cardinals in Rome did not know at first what Pope John XXIII
meant when he announced the desire of an "ecumenical council of
the whole Church." [31] Did he mean a convention of all Christian
churches or would it be a traditional council representing all Catholic
communities from around the world? It was the latter interpretation
that was followed even though observers were invited. In a similar
manner the concept of "dialogue" is open to different definitions.
Typical for Catholic understanding is Congar's publication, *Dialogue
Between Christians: Catholic Contributions to Ecumenism.* [32] Other examples from Congar and Küng indicate that dialogue for them is
not an exchange of ideas with outsiders, but rather a reflection upon

emerging principles from the outside. In this vein, Küng wrote a series of articles for young people during the year 1961 under the title *That the World May Believe*.[33] He writes to an imaginary couple of whom the anonymous male is Catholic and Yvonne is Protestant. The male partner receives a series of counsels concerning abuses and changes in the Church while Yvonne remains the object of concern. He is instructed on how to respond to questions and how to improve his religious life rather than to engage in an exchange of ideas. How can reunion be reached? "By carrying out the justified desires" of the Protestants. The importance of the Scriptures, the position of the laity, and religious freedom are such challenges to tradition Catholicism. Küng concluded: "We ourselves must be firmly believers in order that the world may believe." [34]

Dialogue is then, indeed, an "aggiornamento," a "bringing-up-to-the-present-day" as Küng translated it. Listening to the Protestants and to secular society must serve the cause of self-improvement in order that stumbling blocks may be removed and straying sheep may ultimately come home. Küng has shown himself always a strong believer in the One Holy Roman Catholic Church. It is impressive to witness how Küng later on remained faithful to his Church in spite of conflict and rejection, even in spite of his being relieved from his teaching commission at the University of Tübingen on behalf of the Catholic Church in December of 1979. Hans Küng soundly believes in the institutional Church of which he is a part, however much he is impressed by Protestant theology and secular philosophy. Dialogue, then, can for him only be a temporary antiphony of ideas resounding ultimately in the harmony of the one holy Catholic Church of all ages.

3. *Renewal through Theological Reformulation*

As a historical theologian, Küng is not just concerned about a reinterpretation of history, he also approaches issues from a theological perspective. Also on this level he uses the insights of the latest research and knows how to present his case in an appealing manner. The ecclesiological issue between Rome and the Reformation is discussed by Küng on the basis of the biblical symbol of the "Body of Christ." Since the Reformation, the Pauline texts using this motif have been cherished by the Anabaptists, the Congregationalists, and the Baptists in support of their concept of the priesthood of all believers.[35] Especially the words of 1 Corinthians 12:12b had strong appeal: ". . . all the members of the body, though many, are one body. . . ." According to Gustave Weigel, Catholic theologians had identified the nature of the Church in terms of the "Kingdom of God" concept ever since the first Christian emperor, Constantine the Great. Catholic theology had been more interested in establishing the vertical dimension of hierarchical leadership than the horizontal relations among actual church members.[36]

In response to the Protestant challenge, two Catholic professors at the University of Tübingen, J. A. Möhler and Karl Adam,[37] have stirred admiration and controversy within the Catholic Church by focusing upon the Church as a body of believers. The publications of these professors were almost exactly a century apart, 1825 and 1924, setting the stage for Hans Küng, who became professor of "Fundamental Theology" at the same University of Tübingen in 1960. Even the triumphalist Pope Pius XII stepped in the act by promulgating in 1943 an encyclical on the mystical body of Christ stressing, however, also in this model the vertical dimension of the relation to Christ as the head of the body.[38]

Father Yves Congar infused yet another influence into Küng's ecclesiology. The former's theory is derived from the incarnational model of John 1:14. This allows for the vertical dimension in relation to Christ, but it also provides an opportunity to speak about the limitations of the flesh as they occur in the horizontal relations of actual church life. In precise parallels Congar lists the distinctions between the institutional hierarchy on the one hand and the spiritual communion on the other hand. He sees, however, a vital interaction between these two realms since in Christ both natures are one. "The Church as 'Institution' is the instrument of the Church as 'mystical Body.' " The sacramental Church is at the same time the congregational Church—both are truly one flesh in Christ.[39]

Küng follows the incarnational model in his challenge to the Council, while later his standard work on the Church will make specific applications of the Cornithian model of the Church as the body of Christ. In his incarnational definition of the Church, Küng does not exercise the same caution as Congar and Karl Adam by focusing on the divine nature of the Church. Küng rather uses the dimension of the human nature of Christ as a reference to the limitations of the Church. The local Church or the Church at large has, indeed, for Küng a divine as well as a human dimension, like the incarnate Christ. For Küng, however, the human side has the focus of attention; *there* are the areas of need, ignorance among the laity and neglect among the clergy. To illustrate his point, Küng makes use of the converted Anglican clergyman, John Henry Newman, who became Catholic and in 1879 became a cardinal. In one of his sermons Newman wrote: "The grace of God has but partial possession even of religious men, and the best that can be said of us is, that we have two sides, a light side and a dark, and that the dark happens to be outermost. Thus we form part of the world to each other, though we be not of the world." [40]

In borrowing terminology from Karl Rahner, Hans Küng calls his Church a "sinful Church" or a "Church of sinners." [41] To be sure, sin does not arise from the nature of the Church, but it penetrates the community from the outside. The most visible sins are, of course, the sins of its leaders. "An immoral laity, bad priests, bishops and Popes—these are the saddest wounds of the Body of the mystical Christ." [42] Even if the Church would have neither overt nor covert sins it would still have its shortcomings and would need to be adapted to ever new situations. Küng claims the Church Father Augustine in his earnest concern for reform by quoting from the latter's commentary on Psalm 103: "Do you wish to be pleasing to him [i.e. to Christ]? You cannot, as long as you are deformed. What will you do to be beautiful? First let your deformity be displeasing to yourself, then . . . he will reform you, who first formed you." [43]

Traditionally, Catholic theologians have looked at the Church from above, stressing the divine nature of her hierarchy and her sacraments. As Küng states, this attitude causes an idealist outlook resulting in a neglect of attention for the human deficiencies of the congregational community. The Protestants and the secularists, however, look at the churches from below, perceiving only the sociopolitical powers at work in the ecclesiastical organizations.[44] Like Congar, Küng believes in the interaction of the divine and the human powers within the holy organism of the Church.

Küng is of the opinion that Luther could have avoided the disastrous schism if he would have applied his insight in human nature to the practice and policies of the Church of his day. Luther did believe that even the best Christian remained in need of justifying

grace; his repeated affirmation was that man is simultaneously justified and sinful.[45] Why could Luther not tolerate a "sinful Church"?
Was he like the sectarians, mentioned by Küng, seeking for "a
church of the pure"? [46] Luther certainly was not a Puritan. Even
after he had established control in his Church Luther did not establish
a rigid church discipline; he merely expressed the desire to gather
those "who want to be Christians in earnest and who profess the
Gospel with hand and mouth." [47]

Dr. Rudolph J. Ehrlich in his assessment of Küng's analysis of
Luther, demonstrates that Luther did not just want to purify the
Roman Church from its abuses, which certainly were there. Luther
rather wanted to go at the root of all the abusive evidences. These
roots were the doctrines of salvation, of revelation, and of the
Church.[48] In view of these doctrines, his three "alones" were pro-
posed: "by grace alone," "by Scripture alone," and "by faith alone."
The Protestant Reformers may have concentrated on the Church
as it is seen from below with all its "stains and wrinkles." The
Protestants had, however, a high view of salvation and revelation.
They believed in God's election and illumination; they did not need
the human institutions and channels of grace to convey a message
of grace. The picture is more complex than Küng suggested. The
Catholics may have been idealist triumphalists by looking at the
church merely from above; the Protestants were convinced of *both*
the human as well as the divine perspective of their churches.

Hans Küng reiterates Barth's emphatic confession concerning the
Church. Barth had rejected the preposition "in," which is used in
some Latin versions of the Nicene Creed.[49] It should read "credo
ecclesiam" rather than "credo in ecclesiam," according to Barth.
Both Barth and Küng agree that there should remain a distinction
between believing *in* God, *in* Christ, and *in* the Holy Spirit, and
believing the Church as the body of gathered believers. The Church
cannot claim the final allegiance that God in Christ demands of
His people. Küng seems to agree verbally with Barth on this point.[50]

There remains, however, a basic difference when dealing with
the perfection or infallibility of the Church. When Küng in later
years questions the infallibility of the pope, he professes the infallibility of the Church; the body belongs to Christ; its earthly head represents the body rather than the head, according to Küng.[51] The Church
is already the "bride without spot or wrinkle" as Küng infers from

Ephesians 5:27. It is, indeed, a hidden reality to be revealed only at the end of time. "Holiness is the light of the Church, sinfulness her shadow; holiness reveals her nature, sinfulness obscures it." [52] For Protestant believers, this ideal remains basically an eschatological reality saved for the end of times. For the time being, the Protestant, and especially the evangelical Protestant, focuses on individual salvation, on the living stones by which the Church victorious is being built.

All Christians agree with Küng that renewal and mutual understanding would be greatly helped by going at the theological roots of the tragic divide of the Reformation. Such a dialogue would, however, not be a simplistic polarization of divine and human perspective, of a sacramental and a congregational concept of the Church, of an optimistic triumphalist over against a negative secular concept of the institution of the Church, and, finally, of a view from above in contrast to a view from below. Both Catholics and Protestants have humanist or anthropocentric tendencies; both also believe in the divine perspective of their communion, and both can use in good conscience the incarnational model for their ecclesiology. The difference between these two forms of Christianity is rather in the view of the function of the institution itself. For the Protestants it is not part of the order of salvation; [53] they have a lower view of the Church even though most of them could still say after Barth: "I believe the Church."

4. Renewal through Self-Evaluation

In his first translated publication, *The Council, Reform and Reunion,* Küng proved to be an ardent defender of the Roman Catholic faith. His strength was not in historical analysis nor in the theological formulations that he largely borrowed from predecessors,[54] but rather in presenting the positive elements of his faith. In his early years, Küng was basically an apologist for the Roman Catholic Church. Fifteen years later, he demonstrated his abilities as apologist for Christianity in general by his German best-seller, *On Being a Christian* (1974).

Küng was easily challenged to a response to criticism. While in Rome as a student, he was confronted by Barth and Hegel and immediately decided to tackle these giants of the non-Catholic camp.

A similar challenge took place in Tübingen where Küng encountered
the persuasive New Testament scholar, Ernst Käsemann, who confronted Küng with the New Testament development of the church
thus far unknown to him. "I buried myself in the relevant literature
and also discussed the question intensively with my Catholic colleague. . . ." [55] A year later, Küng had incorporated his new insights
in an article for a professional journal. It had the title " 'Early
Catholicism' in the New Testament as a Problem in Controversial
Theology." [56] During the same year, Küng presented this subject
to the bishops and theologians gathered in Rome at the occasion
of the first session of Vatican II. More examples can be given where
Küng digested a new idea in a relatively brief time using it then
for an enthusiastic apology for his Church.[57]

As advocate for the Roman Church, Küng wanted to correct first
of all the impression that reform is the prerogative of Protestantism
only. Küng rightly demonstrates that through all ages of the Christian
era the Church has been subjected to changes and adjustments. Already in biblical times a council was held to liberate the churches
from the burden of Jewish Christian legalism as is vividly described
in Acts 15. During the centuries following, the churches had to
adjust their worship to a variety of missionary situations. Soon the
Scriptures had been translated into Syriac, Coptic, Ethiopian, Arme-
nian, and into a number of other languages. The Latin Vulgate was
the result of one such adaptation; its translation was commissioned
to the scholarly monk, Jerome, by Pope Damasis I. Küng continues
to list the variety of reforms and changes during the first millennium
of the Christian era and succeeds in portraying a dynamic Christian
movement.[58]

The question should be raised, however: Can a Roman Catholic
apologist simply claim as evidences for the inner strength of Roman
Christianity the New Testament, the Eastern churches, the Arian
missionaries Cyril and Methodius, and even the anti-Roman Iro-Scot-
tish monks? Küng attempts, indeed, to prove a similar dynamic
during the medieval Western Church under Rome's leadership. There
certainly were great spiritual leaders like Bernard of Clairvaux and
Francis of Assisi. These great monastic leaders were, however, more
"renewers" than "reformers." They did not introduce new forms
of church order nor did they attempt any theological articulation.
The monastic leaders evoked a host of spiritual renewal movements
but these were of secondary importance since they had no "far-

reaching success." [59] It is true that popes and councils can be mentioned in the endeavor to halt the abuses spreading in the medieval Church.[60] Küng must concede, however, that "all the *official* attempts at reforming the Church in these centuries dwindled equally into despair . . . because . . . they did not embark boldly on any radical reform but stuck fast on superficialities." [61] Six months after the Fifth, and last, Lateran Council the ninety-five theses were posted by Luther and "reform had come with a vengeance." [62]

These last quotes indicate that Küng does not simply want to advocate the Catholic Church of the past nor of the present. He wants to be a mediating apologist explaining to both parties involved in the conflict what the causes of estrangement were and continued to be up until the present. After attempting to demonstrate that reform is not foreign to Catholic Christianity, Küng proceeds to explain the process of overreaction in the Roman Catholic community. The Protestants called it the movement of "Counter Reformation" while Küng speaks of a ghetto mentality resulting in a defense against Protestantism and other modern movements. "Catholics of the nineteenth century, particularly in Germany, suffered from a multiple inferiority complex in face of the achievements of Protestantism at that date." [63] Already Congar had pointed to the "perils of prophecy" in his study on "True and False Reform." Congar asserted that the intrepid challenge of prophets like Luther placed the leaders of the establishment on the defense.[64] Thus, Küng had accused the Reformers of actually provoking "a certain anthropocentricity" among the leaders of the Council of Trent,[65] who were gathered to refute the theology of the Reformation during the years of 1545 to 1563.

This attitude of defensiveness and isolationism culminated in the nineteenth century when Pope Pius IX issued the infamous "Syllabus of Errors" that rejected eighty forms of contemporary ideologies. In consequence, the popes were perceived as "anti-national, anti-democratic, anti-lay, anti-social, and anti-liberal" by the Germans.[66] Even Protestant Bible societies were rejected as erroneous ventures. As a result, the Catholics themselves were all too often led to a restriction of Bible reading.[67] Indirectly the Protestants have caused this attitude of defensiveness, according to Küng. Even the definition of the dogma of papal infallibility in the year 1870 can be seen as the ultimate consequence of "the exigencies of defensive warfare." [68]

Küng argues, however, that the Catholics have experienced a continuing renewal also after the Reformation. The Council of Trent was not merely a defensive reaction; it also carried out reforms not suggested by Luther or Calvin. It dealt, for instance, with disciplinary decrees concerning marriage, the education of the clergy, and the duties of the bishops. There was no lack of charismatic leaders during the post-Reformation era; Ignatius of Loyola founded the militant Jesuit order, Teresa of Avila inspired the deep spirituality of the Carmelites, and the devout scientist, Blaise Pascal, was venerated by Protestants as well as Catholics. Even during the reactionary nineteenth century, Küng can point to alert theologians like his predecessor in Tübingen, J. A. Möhler. During that same century the widely publicized Anglican scholar, John H. Newman, joined the Roman Catholic Church and was appointed cardinal by Pope Leo XIII.[69] The same pope was first to address the Protestants as "beloved" or "separated brothers." During the rule of this pope, the Vatican archives were opened to scholars of all nations and creeds. According to Pope Leo XIII, "the Church has nothing to fear from truth." [70] Even private Bible reading in the vernacular was encouraged after years of negative interventions.

Yet, Küng exclaimed: "What a difference between the Church in 1878, when Leo XIII became Pope, and 1958, when John XXIII became Pope! . . . the Catholic Church of 1961 is in whole areas of her life a reformed and renewed Catholic Church." [71] Küng proudly presents his Church with its rich inheritance of spirituality, theology, and leadership. Audiences throughout the English-speaking world would soon respond to the enthusiasm of the junior spokesman of the Catholic Church. At age thirty-four, Küng began his first six-week tour through the United States and England. Numerous world-wide tours followed and everywhere he encountered a similar enthusiastic response. Küng's mediating apologetics challenged Catholics and Protestants alike; he was welcomed especially during the sixties when no need was felt to perpetuate the old religious establishments. A refutation of the past and dedication to social issues united men and women from a variety of religious backgrounds. Later developments, however, have indicated that such spontaneity did not weather the test of time. The agony and tears of centuries of conflict could not simply be cast off like a burdensome yoke, however comfortable that would be for the parties involved. Küng himself would have to experience that the hard way!

5. Renewal through Accommodation

The quest for reconciliation had been prepared ever since the ministry of Pope Leo XIII (1878–1903). This pope had suggested an annual nine-day period of prayer for reconciliation among Christians already in the year 1895. Thirteen years later, a prayer octave was instituted by Brother Paul of Graymoor in Lyons, France, and continued by Paul Couturier. Parallel to these devotional movements was the ecumenical work of Yves Congar. For him the central objective of Catholic ecumenism would be the reincorporation of "all genuine Christian values dispersed through the world." [72] Any "spiritual values, in so far as they are positive, actually belong to the Catholic Church," [73] according to Congar. The Catholics as well as the Protestants would be blessed by this "reincorporation" of the separated brethren, although this "reintegration of dissidents would bring nothing new to the Church; on the contrary, it is they who would be the gainers." [74] The model of the "seamless robe" [75] that had been torn up by schismatics and heretics asks for a "reunion" rather than a process of reconciliation.

Even though Küng follows the model of Congar to a great extent, he is more open to confess shortcomings as well as to acknowledge insight gained from Protestantism. "We are not obliged to act before the world as though everything were the best with us. We can display our poverty, our wretchedness, our shame." [76] His model of the Church is rather that of a fortress that has been deserted by some of its best troops.[77] Küng, indeed, wants a homecoming, but then in the form of a reconciliation. "Reunion will then neither be a Protestant 'return' nor a Catholic 'capitulation,' but a brotherly approach from both sides." [78] Both parties would agree to cooperate in the effort to proclaim the message of Christ so "That the World May Believe," as the title of his series to young people ran during those early years.[79] Küng is strongly convinced, though, that the Catholics hold the fort, even though the runaway militia may own the talent and the skills.[80]

The encounter between the faithful and the runaways is not meant as a value judgment, though. Küng compares the two parties with the sons of Zebedee competing for the most honorable place in the Kingdom. Both sides have their fallacies; both Catholics as well as Protestants will have to confess their share in the disastrous schism.[81] The Catholics need to become aware of how they have ignored Protestantism all through the nineteenth century and how they have kept the truth hidden by not encouraging the laity to read the Scriptures.[82] Their scholars ought to reveal how even a genuine confession by Pope Adrian VI at the Diet of Ratisbon (1522–23) went ignored for four hundred years.[83] All Catholics ought to unite in common confession, according to Küng, but so do the Protestants.

Küng alerts the Protestants to the danger of calling themselves churches of the Reformation or Reformed Churches, as if the process of reform for them has been completed. "Might not this too be self-glorifying and self-righteous Pharisaism, even though it were accompanied by prayer?" he asks rhetorically.[84] Küng quotes in this connection the Swiss Reformed theologian, Hermann Kutter, who wrote: "I believe that if Luther and Zwingli were to rise from their graves today, they would drive us from our building sites and say: 'We know you not, for all your fine centenary essays and Reformation celebrations. You are not Protestants, you make no protest of your own, you only keep celebrating ours.' " [85] Reunion for Küng involves adjustment or accommodation on both sides, a willingness to grow together in faith, worship, and action.

The Dominican scholar, Yves Congar, set the parameters of such a rapprochement between the Catholic Church and the Protestant or the secular world. Carefully he had analyzed what a true reformer should do and what makes for a "false reformer" or a schismatic revolutionary. As the four requirements for true reform, Congar listed first of all the priority of pastoral concern exemplified by a monastic leader like Francis of Assisi.[86] Congar discussed three additional requirements that are actually further elaborations of his basic theme of pastoral reform. The additional requirements are solidarity with the religious community, an attitude of patience without retardation, and, finally, a method of development rather than of innovation.[87] All four of these requirements for sound reform point to a process of continuity rather than discontinuity, an approach that was endorsed by Pope John XXIII and consequently by Vatican II.

Küng's other "fatherly friend," Karl Barth, caricatures the traditional Catholic attitude toward reform. Küng has preserved Barth's observations in the following quote taken from Küng's messages to young people.

> You Catholics are strange people! If any of you ever does manage to see that there's anything awry in your Church, or downright rotten,

and even if he goes so far as to admit that it's so, then—well, what does he do then? He takes a deep breath, swallows the nasty mouthful down, digests it in a trice, and says, 'But I'm still a Catholic all the same!' And nothing else happens at all.[88]

Küng, then, was confronted with the alternative of his two "fatherly friends," [89] with a process of continuity over against an attitude of crisis and discontinuity. Barth demonstrated this attitude vividly by his decisive participation in the secession of the Confessing Church from the German Christians who wanted to remain loyal to the commencing Hitler regime in 1934.

Küng attempted to find a compromise between Congar's pastoral approach and Barth's prophetic stance. Küng is, therefore, more eager than Congar to remove certain traditions, customs, or concepts that create conflict between Catholics and Protestants. Some of the major stumbling blocks are the role of the pope and the position of Mary, which issues ultimately relate to the whole concept of the Church.[90] Küng's next project would be a detailed study of the Church that will be discussed in the next chapter. The following stage in Küng's reforming activities would be a redefining of the pope's position in the Church, which would get him involved in an inextricable conflict with his own community. As most progressive Catholics have slighted the issue of Mariology, so Küng has not devoted much energy to this question. He hoped that on this point the Protestants would yield and develop a greater reverence for Mary who after all was declared by Scripture as "blessed among the women." "In . . . Marian devotion . . . the sin of excess is not the only possible one; there is . . . a sin by neglect as well. And as we do not spare ourselves in our examination of conscience, so our Protestant brethren cannot spare themselves either." [91]

The time seemed ready, then, for Küng and many others that the Christian churches of the world could remove the barriers between them and march together so "That the World May Believe," as the title ran of Küng's messages in the early sixties. The sounds and hopes of those tumultuous years have, however, been smothered by the raucous voices of war, economic deprivation of third world countries, and nuclear armament of the superpowers. Within his own ecclesiastical community Küng now stands at the sidelines. Was he, together with other progressive Catholics, too eager to solve within a matter of years the problems accumulated over several centuries? A radical change could have come, as it once did during the years of Luther's life. At this time, it is still difficult to distinguish clearly all the cultural, social, and religious forces in world history that so decisively determined the development of the churches in the sixties. Christians can only deplore the lack of historical insight of Catholic historians in general and of Küng in particular.

The conflict of the sixteenth century was much wider in scope than the issue of the supposedly rebellious monk, Luther. Küng shows no familiarity with the audacious Puritan movement reaching out to the Americas; he has no sense for the electrifying movements of Pietist revivalism that also claimed the Reformation as their base; Küng does not have a high esteem for evangelical Protestantism and its missionary embrace of the world during the nineteenth century; Küng never quotes a gospel song or hymn that has carried the message in a nonverbal and nonliturgical manner in a way Erasmus once predicted during the sixteenth century.[92] Did Küng have a vision of the actual aggiornamento needed for the Church of Rome? Would it not have been appropriate to speak at least once about a divine judgment over the corruptions of medieval Europe? For the Protestants, Luther, Zwingli, Calvin, John Knox, and many other great leaders were just instruments in God's hand. Any one of those leaders could have been missed and the radical change of reform would still have taken place. History has its divine dimension incorporating the qualities but also the failures of men. Luther certainly had his human weaknesses, but God used these. A valid vision of history should be alert to the human *and* the divine aspects. No rapprochement between Catholics and Protestants seems likely without a thorough historical and theological study of the persons and factors involved.

IV
The Church

1. The Issue

From his hotel room Hans Küng could see the huge dome of St. Peter's. After days of hesitation he had made up his mind.[1] In competition with the Vatican Fathers busily gathering, he would write a major work on the Church from a biblical perspective in order to balance this insight with the power struggle in progress in the Vatican. Already in 1937, his mentor, Karl Barth, had voiced the opinion that all issues between Rome and Reformation, even the papacy and the sacraments, were negotiable when agreement could be reached on the nature of the Church.[2] For years, Küng had cherished a quiet admiration for Karl Adam, one of his Catholic predecessors in Tübingen, who had written a classic and widely accepted ecclesiology.[3] It had been the first of its kind in Catholic tradition. In anticipation of the Council, Küng himself had written a historical study on *Structures of the Church*.[4] Additional inspiration on the issue of the Church had been received from his senior Protestant colleagues in Tübingen, Ernst Käsemann and Hermann Diem.[5] Moved by a variety of factors, defiance of the Vatican Fathers, admiration for his mentors Adam and Barth, stimulation by his senior colleagues in Tübingen, and, ultimately, by his own aspirations, Küng set to work in the quietness of his hotel room during the fall of 1963.

By 1967, Küng's popular publication on *The Church* rolled off the presses in Germany, Holland, and England.[6] From a perspective of time, Küng had lost his competition since all the documents by the Vatican commissions had been formulated and accepted by the end of 1965.[7] As far as publicity was concerned, however, Küng had won the contest. Many members of the clergy and laity agreed with Küng that a more democratic and biblical approach to the Church was the most relevant issue in the late sixties. The sensitivity of the issue was demonstrated by the immediate reaction of the chairman of the Theological Commission, Cardinal Ottaviani. Already during the Christmas season of 1967, he "ordered" Küng to stop further distribution of his book. Instead, Küng responded by accelerating the process of translating the book in still other languages. Ever since the first session of Vatican II, Küng had developed a conscious antagonism against this conservative cardinal who headed the controversial Theological Commission. It was because of Ottaviani's intransigent leadership that Küng had resigned his position in the Commission just before he began writing his book on the Church.[8] In a very realistic way, Küng had experienced the tensions between administrators and advisors, between bishops and "periti," as they were called during Vatican II. Küng was going to demonstrate the difference between historical pragmatism and biblical idealism in matters of the Church.

A decisive turn of events had taken place between the two sessions of 1962 and 1963. The sudden death of Pope John XXIII in June of 1963 had caused a considerable shift of power from the progressives to the conservatives, i.e., from leaders like Küng to cardinals like Ottaviani. The unique leadership of Pope John had been an inspiration to all participants in the Vatican Council. With great enthusiasm, Küng had recorded his daily impressions in his diary, *The Council in Action.*[9] He had been challenged particularly by the genuine candor of the eighty-year-old pope "beaming with simplicity, amiability and deep affection." [10] Especially the pope's intervention on behalf of the bishops against the prestigious Theological Commission had incited Küng's enthusiasm. The Commission was requested to restudy its schema on revelation and to coordinate its effort with the Secretariat for Christian Unity.[11] Among the new members elected was also Hans Küng, who eagerly articulated the latest insights of German theology in biblical and historical orientation in connection with the issues of revelation and the Church.

Küng boldly spoke to national caucuses of bishops or he gathered discussion groups around him in the Vatican coffee-bar. By his critics Küng was called a "theological teen-ager"; [12] among the aged Church leaders Küng must have been in striking contrast, being only thirty-four years old himself. Following this exhilarating fall season came Küng's first tour through the United States. Then Pope John XXIII died and with his successor, Pope Paul VI, a time of stabilization began. When the Council convened again during the fall of 1963, Küng had the temerity to question the make-up of the Theological Commission. He particularly took issue with the chairmanship of Cardinal Ottaviani, who had not been elected by the bishops, but appointed by the Curia.[13] The favorable time for Küng was over, however; his request was ignored, and Küng felt obligated to resign under those circumstances. The Church was retracing its steps, and the relationship between the Vatican and its rebellious prophet would rapidly deteriorate until the final breaking point in 1979.[14]

The course of events demonstrated clearly to Küng that the major issue had become the nature of the Church itself. Was it a merely administrative hierarchical organization or was it a representation of the people of God? If it has both aspects, how do these interrelate? When Küng began writing his book on the Church, he was understandably in a reactionary mood. As Luther once did, so Küng began to question the historical development of the Roman Catholic Church. He had hoped for a more democratic or rather charismatic development of the contemporary Church as he had laid down in his exposition on the *Structures of the Church*. With the enthronement of Pope Paul VI a more institutionally oriented Church had returned. For Küng, the New Testament as well as the history of the Church clearly demonstrated a more charismatic pattern of the Church consisting in active participation by the laity, by the theologians, and even by the rulers. Especially since the Council of Trent, institutional clericalism had been on the increase, reaching its culmination in the First Vatican Council of 1870.[15] The ecclesiological question had gradually become an inner-Catholic issue. Küng found himself in the midst of a struggle of the competing forces of charisma and institution, between the theologians and the bishops, the progressive

Church and the triumphalist Church, the young generation and the old leaders. Küng's critical approach to the institutional church was welcomed by the progressive young Catholics and by Protestants.

Küng begins his book by questioning the permanence of historical forms. "The Church can become a prisoner of the image it has made for itself at one particular period in history." "The 'essence' of the Church . . . exists in constantly changing historical 'forms.' " [16] With these statements in his opening chapter, Küng takes a critical stance toward those who believe in a linear evolvement of the historical Church, which has been the accepted theory of the Roman Catholic Church. Even Congar had argued for a reform in the sense of a consistent development, thereby rejecting any incongruous innovations.[17]

Küng raises the scriptural origin of the Church as the only norm for later historical forms, which allows him to be more radical than any of his coreligionists. Küng rejects both the traditionalist and the modernist approach; the traditionalist follows uncritically the culture of the past, while the modernist is "enslaved by the present age or culture." [18] Küng wants to follow the Protestant principle of a return to the Scriptures. The new perspective is, however, that Küng finds the Catholic as well as the Protestant model in the various New Testament writings. His ideal of the Church is a challenge to the Catholic traditionalists and modernists as well as to the Protestants. According to Küng, the question of the Church is an issue for all Christians.

2. The Kingdom of God

For his comprehensive study of the Church, Küng subjects the New Testament models of the Church to a thorough linguistic and contextual investigation. The first and major emphasis is given to the Church as the "Kingdom of God," [19] because it establishes the transcendent origin of the Church that precedes and overrules all human organization. The Greek term, "basileia theou," occurs a hundred times in the Synoptic Gospels, which is an indication of its early use by Jesus and his disciples. By contrast, the term "ekklesia," which is commonly translated by the word "church," occurs only twice in the Gospels, namely in Matthew 16:18 and 18:17.[20] Though traditionally the concepts "kingdom" and "church" have been closely identified by Catholic theologians,[21] Küng sets out to elaborate the theological difference between these terms.

> While ekklesia is something essentially of the present, something finite, basileia is something which, although it has irrupted into the present, belongs fundamentally to the future. . . . Ekklesia embraces sinners and righteous, basileia is the kingdom of the righteous, of the saints. Ekklesia grows from below, can be organized, is the product of development and progress and dialectic, in short is definitely the work of man; basileia comes from above, is an unprepared action, an incalculable event, in short is definitely the work of God.[22]

The distinction enunciated by Küng is generally indicated by the dialectic of visible and invisible Church. Küng accepts the dialectic, but he resolutely rejects a simplistic identification of the visible Church and God's Kingdom. Disapprovingly he quotes the sixteenth-century Cardinal Bellarmine who considered the "Church to be as visible as the republic of Venice." [23] Küng rather takes sides with the Reformers and their forerunners, Wycliffe and Huss, who opposed "the idea that the Church was simply the all too visible institution of the medieval Church." [24] These reformers started from the invisible nature of the Church and proclaimed its visible manifestation not in a sacred institution but rather "in the preaching of the word and in the administering of the sacraments, and also in the community's confession of faith." [25]

The concept of the "Kingdom of God" indicates the historical dimension of the Church embracing the past, the present, and the future. Catholics may glory in their past and Protestants may dwell on the present, but both Catholics and Protestants have been negligent of the future fulfillment of the Kingdom. Küng draws upon Albert Schweitzer and Karl Barth in emphasizing the eschatological message of the gospel. Barth stated in his *Letter to the Romans:* "Christianity which is not totally and entirely eschatology has separated itself totally and entirely from Christ." [26]

Following the salvation history school of Oscar Cullmann and the Catholic scholar, Rudolf Schnackenburg, Küng considers the Kingdom of God from the aspects of past and present as well as future. "Jesus' preaching of the reign of God is at once an expectation of the future and a proclamation of the present." [27] Küng uses the eschatological dimension especially to tone down the triumphalist spirit of the sixties. "The Church may be termed the fellowship of aspirants to the Kingdom of God. . . . The meaning of the Church does not reside in itself, in what it is, but in what it is moving towards." [28] This does not mean that Küng would be unmindful of the historical Church, but its value lies not in the institution but rather in its connection with the decisive events of redemption. The Church is merely a pilgrim church having "the resurrection not only ahead of it, but in its decisive form behind it: in Jesus the risen Kyrios." [29]

Küng is well aware of the fact that he has to distinguish his eschatological approach from the visions of the utopian dreamers in Christianity. He decisively rejects the medieval monastic leader, Joachim of Flora, who announced the imminent advent of the era of the Holy Spirit. Also, the Protestant radical reformer, Thomas Müntzer, is rejected for his social millennarianism. According to Küng, these and other utopian movements have lost a respect for the past, they "were radically anti-ecclesiastical." [30] A healthy eschatological existence should have a high esteem for historical Christianity. With this affirmative attitude in mind, Küng quoted the seemingly cynical remark by the French Catholic modernist, Alfred Loisy: "Jesus proclaimed the Kingdom of God, and what came was the Church." [31] Adopting this perception positively, Küng affirms that the vision of Christ had to take concrete historical form. The contemporary Christian can have a constructive vision only against the backdrop of historical Christianity. The historical institution of the Church does have its divine and its human aspects; it is a church of saints as well as a church of sinners. These two aspects must remain in dialectical tension. They can never be identified nor totally be separated.[32] "For the Christian the Church is primarily there not to be admired nor to be criticized but to be believed." [33]

Thus, the Church is an object of faith or of dependence on the leadership of the Holy Spirit. The translations for the term *ekklesia* indicate such a dependence clearly. The Gothic word *kuriký* is used by the German translation "Kirche," by the English "Church" or the Scottish "kirk." The Greek root *ekklesia* was transliterated by the Latin *ecclesia* or the French *église*. [34] Whichever rendering is followed, both point beyond themselves to the God who is calling (*ekklesia*) or to the Christ who is sanctifying (*kuriký*). Thus, the Christians are called the elect or the saints. Because of its divine origin, the Christian community is frequently called the "Church of God" in the New Testament.[35] Clearly, the Christian Church is not the product of an international or a local organization. The new community was born after the resurrection event through the outpouring of the Holy Spirit. "The Church sprang not from imaginations, not out of baseless credulity, but from real experiences of encounters with one who was truly alive." [36] Küng repudiates both the universal institutionalism of the Catholic Church and democratic Congregationalism in the Protestant wing. "The Church is not composed by the free association of individuals; it is more than the sum of its members." [37] The Kingdom of God has to be received in an attitude of repentance that requires a total inward change of the entire man.[38] The frequent use of the concept of the Kingdom of God in the New Testament indicates that the origin of the Church is foremost from above; it is, therefore, the object of repentant faith.

The concept of the "Kingdom of God" provided Küng with a vantage point from which to evaluate both Catholic and Protestant ecclesiology. The former may glory in its visible historical institution, and the latter may be satisfied with the invisible universal community of believers. Both need the vision of the future fulfillment of the Kingdom. To live for the future Church as the "bride without spot or wrinkle" would mean a coming together as Protestants and Catholics in a confession of guilt and in a profession of faith. It would mean a willingness to change traditional forms and methods to always preserve a high esteem for historical structures. It would mean a radical turn—a "metanoia"—by Church leaders and theologians in order to respond to the call from above. Küng is challenged by the prophets and, in his *Structures of the Church*, he identifies the role of the theologian with the prophetic voice in the Church.[39] There is a dialectic interaction between the *basileia theou* and the *ekklesia*. In his *Structures of the Church*, Küng discusses in detail the interaction of divine and human vocation in the Church, its councils and its ministry.[40] Since the Kingdom precedes the *ekklesia* in time and in meaning, the prophet should have at least a place of equality with the sacerdotal leader.

3. The Church of God

The invisible Kingdom of God has become historical reality in the *ekklesia* of God's people. Jesus proclaimed the *basileia theou* and, after his resurrection, the *ekklesia* came into being.[41] The New Testament writers used the term "people of God" for the members of the *ekklesia*. According to Küng, the identity given by the early Christians was not "disciples" nor even "Christians," but first and foremost that of the "people of God." [42] By this name they claimed to be part of the great history of salvation, and took its beginning in the call of the fathers Abraham, Isaac, and Jacob. Israel was the chosen people of God, but since they had rejected Jesus as their Messiah, the Christians felt that they continued the covenantal relation with God in a new manner.[43] Thus, the apostle Paul could quote the prophet Hosea with confidence: "Those who were not my people I will call 'my people.'" James, the leader of the Jewish Christians, concurred: "God has visited the Gentiles, to take out of them a people for his name." [44] This identity was made concrete by the initiation of baptism, by the celebration the eschatological meal, by the repeating of the Lord's Prayer together, by the following of the apostles' teaching, and by the living of a fellowship of love.[45] The early Christians were strengthened in the awareness of being this new people of God, especially in the book of Hebrews. They were the "New Israel" because Christ was their great high priest and salvation was granted to all who obeyed him, to the Jews as well as to the Gentiles.[46]

The implications of this characterization of the Church are far-reaching, according to Küng. In the first place, the later development of a division between clergy and laity is incompatible with the concept of the "people of God." To belong to this new people was more important than any other distinction of service or leadership. The terms clergy and laity did not exist and do not occur in the New Testament, even though both terms have Greek roots.[47] To be a citizen of the New Israel or a child of God could only be distinguished from noncitizens or non-Christians who were slaves of sin.[48] Küng is of the opinion that this early Christian identity can be revived. In his book, *On Being a Christian*, he further describes the challenge of being a mature Christian in the Church and in contemporary society.

A second implication of the appellation of the "people of God" is the question of the Jews and their relation to the new covenant. Küng accuses the Church in general of having misunderstood the apostle Paul who, in his letter to the Romans (chapters 9–11), discussed the rejection of Israel as temporary until the fullness of the Gentiles would be achieved. The medieval Church and postmedieval Christianity have persecuted the Jews in a sometimes gruesome manner with the help of secular rulers. Küng does not hesitate to mention that Catholic commentators on the Nazi race laws appealed to their "unshakable faith that they were acting in accordance with the will of the omnipotent creator." [49] The rationalization for this anti-Semitic behavior was that all the judgments and curses of the Old Testament pertained to the Jews, while all the promises and blessings were inherited by the Christians. Küng also makes mention of the declaration by Vatican II on the new relation to the Jews. It states: "The Church repudiates all persecutions against any man. Moreover, mindful of her common patrimony with the Jews . . . she deplores the hatred, persecutions and displays of anti-Semitism directed against the Jews at any time and from any source." [50] Küng wants more than repentance, though. He wants some form of cooperation with the Jews presenting the secular world with the good news of the Kingdom of God. In the process of this common challenge, the Church is to "make Israel jealous" as the apostle Paul states in Romans 11:11 and 14. The new people of God are related to the old people as the younger son to the older son in Jesus' parable in Luke 15. Both sons have the same Father in Heaven. [51]

The community of Christians is described variously as the royal priesthood, the chosen race, or as the temple of God. The most unique, however, is Paul's image of the Church as the "body of Christ." According to Küng, there are no Hebrew equivalents for this use of the word "body," nor has any other New Testament author made use of it. [52] The major passages of the Church as the body of Christ occur in the primary letters of Paul, namely: Romans 12, 1 Corinthians 12, Colossians 1, and Ephesians 4. According to New Testament scholars, the Corinthian passage is among the oldest documents of the canon. What makes these Paulinic passages so unique for Küng is the fact that there are no references to the act of ordination nor to the offices of bishop and elder. [53] The apostle Paul speaks simply about the charismas bestowed upon each of the members of the body in varying degrees. There are distinctions between apostles, teachers, prophets, evangelists, and other forms of service, but "the Pauline Churches did not at all events produce a 'ruling class,' an aristocracy of those endowed with the Spirit who separated themselves from the community and rose above it in order to rule over it." [54]

The way to such an institutionalization is found in the pastoral letters, where the term charisma is only used twice and then in connection with ordination. "Do not neglect the 'charisma' you have, which was given you by prophetic utterance when the elders laid their hands upon you" (1 Timothy 4:14).[55] The Book of Acts represents the same late period of canonic literature; it refers to the laying on of hands but never to the charismas.[56] Küng criticizes the Catholic Church for using only the pastoral letters and Acts as the model for their Church order. The charismatic structure of the early Christian communities is considered obsolete, while it rather should have "a primacy of originality . . . because of its temporal closeness to the Gospel of Jesus." [57] Küng rejects, however, Käsemann's extolling of Paulinic Christianity at the expense of later New Testament forms of so-called "Early Catholicism." The whole New Testament should be the norm for faith and order. Leadership functions did become more pronounced as the Church progressed, but the backdrop of all the services and vocations were the charismas, the gifts by the Spirit, given to all.[58]

Küng observes that the image of the body of Christ makes it possible for Paul to associate with the body of Christ on the cross, the body being broken at the Lord's Supper, and the uniting with the body of Christ in baptism.[59] Even though Küng gives very little attention to the ordinances, he makes some significant observations about their New Testament antecedents.[60] Küng remarks that in the early days public profession of faith was part of the act of baptism, because it was "an action which proclaims and which demands the response of faith." He adds to this that "baptism probably always meant total immersion." [61] Even though Küng portrays the New Testament as a normative ideal for contemporary Christianity he gives no directions for its implementation. In this connection he could have given some credit to the Anabaptists of the Reformation for their courageous attempt to restore the New Testament ordinances. Instead, he accuses them in a different context of trying to "unhistorically return to the Church's origin." In that same general context Küng remarks: "We cannot copy (the New Testament) today, but we can and must translate it into modern terms." [62] Following this hermeneutic, Küng fares a little better with his brief discussion of the Lord's Supper. He rejects the terms "eucharist" and "mass" as being incompatible with the simple New Testament celebration. He does not use the word sacrament for the elements of communion, but rather calls them "an effective sign," "a visible word," or "a real and effective presence" of the Lord.[63] For Küng, the Lord's Supper is first of all a vertical communion with the risen Lord and, horizontally, an eschatological meal of fellow Christians confirming their covenantal relationship in Christ.[64]

As the eschatological orientation inherent to the idea of the Kingdom of God could lead to unbridled utopianism so the charismatic approach has led to movements of excessive enthusiasm. The term itself composed of *en* and *theos* points to an experience of being transported into lofty emotion. The gospel of John with its frequent references to the Spirit has been abused by enthusiasts of all stripes; especially its concept of the paraclete guiding into all truth became an incentive to find ecstatic or mystic insight into the mysteries of life. The early Church attempted to overcome such vagaries "with the help of creeds, a scriptural canon and a reinforced ecclesiastical office," according to Küng.[65] Nonetheless, movements of religious enthusiasm continued over the centuries among Catholics as well as among Protestants. In spite of an impressive bibliographical footnote[66] Küng is not well versed in the history of the radical Reformation. In a broad sweep, he ranges the Baptists, the Quakers, the Plymouth Brethen, the Revivalists, the Mormons, and the contemporary Pentecostalists among expressions of religious enthusiasm.[67] Even though all these groups were against the established religion of their day, they were not necessarily ecstatic or mystic in their orientation.

In all fairness, credit must be given to Küng's objective presentation when he refers to the revival of hagiography and Mariolatry since the time of the Reformation. Also among these movements was a hunger for special revelations and a search for mystic enthusiasm. Küng justly observes that the Bible as well as Christ was overshadowed by these religious aberrations. "It is striking how rarely Christ appeared in all these 'revelations,' 'apparitions' and 'wonders.' "[68] In quite non-Catholic fashion, Küng asserts that only through the power of preaching from the Word of God can such excessive movements of enthusiasm be stemmed.[69] Even though the creed and the ecclesiastical office were among the original means

of counteracting enthusiasm, Küng apparently sees no hope for these
at the present time. His anticlerical mood and his admiration for
Protestantism lead him to side exclusively with the *sola scriptura*
of the Reformation. Küng concludes unambiguously: "The Spirit
of God, if domiciled in the Church, is not domesticated in it. He
is and remains the free Spirit of the free Lord not only of the 'holy
city,' not only of Church offices, not only of the Catholic Church,
not only of Christians, but of the whole world." [70]

4. The Unity of the Church

Where is the true Church? The Kingdom of God is represented
by a great variety of local churches within the community of the
Roman Catholics as well as among the Protestants of different persua-
sions. Variety, however, should be distinguished from particularism,
according to Küng. Variety of religious experience emerging from
a soil of common commitment to Christ is creative, while stubborn
particularism may evoke the rise of heresies.[71] In order to combat
divisiveness the early Church established already during the Council
of Nicaea (A.D. 325) four marks of the Church. The Nicene Creed
reads: "We believe in one, holy, Catholic and Apostolic Church."
At that time the term "Catholic" was still synonymous with the
concept "ecumenical." [72]

The marks of the true Church were used more or less effectively
against heresy and dissension. When major conflicts were raised,
however, by men like John Huss and Martin Luther these classical
marks of the Church were upheld against them in vain; the Western
Catholic Church went through radical divisions. The older churches
adopted the name *Roman* Catholic Church,[73] while the younger
churches received the name "Protestants" during the Augsburg Diet
in 1530. In their Augsburg Confession, the Protestant leaders, represented by Philipp Melanchton, stated: "The Church is . . . the community of saints, in which the pure Gospel is preached and the
sacraments properly administered." [74] The classic marks of the
Church were not rejected but simply considered insufficient. The
Protestant leaders knew from experience that the marks of unity,
holiness, Catholicity, and apostolicity were not necessarily a solid
base for the true Church. So they claimed sound preaching and
the appropriate use of the sacraments as the primary criteria for
the Church.

Hans Küng in his assumed role of mediator between the two blocks of Western Christianity wants to merge the six principles: "The four signs, if they are genuine ones, must in any case depend upon the two others: the unity, holiness, catholicity and apostolicity of the Church do not mean anything if they are not based on the pure Gospel message, valid baptism, and the proper celebration of the Lord's Supper." [75] While the original Catholic marks of the Church are largely verifiable and objective, the Protestant criteria are more theological and subjective in nature. A combination of these two polarities would lead to "evangelical Catholicity," as Küng calls it. [76]

Küng rejects mere external unity as egalitarianism or totalitarianism. [77] He equally repudiates a Catholicity that claims merely numerical quantity or geographic extensity. "Maximal membership, bought at the price of spiritual devaluation and a resultant Christianity of tradition and convention is of no value." [78] Also, the temporal continuity of the apostolic succession does not validate an institution as God's Church. In agreement with the Protestant marks of the Church, it ought to be first of all a "spiritual" community. By this dimension of spirituality Küng means a common acceptance of Jesus Christ as Savior, obedience to the ordinances of baptism and the Lord's Supper, and a biblical proclamation of the Word. [79]

Such a Church is built on the local level from below rather than by a centralist hierarchy from above. It involves common people working together in times of need and supporting one another in situations of persecution. [80] As the early Church developed out of the variety of local churches so the contemporary Church should allow for the infinite multiplicity of local congregations. In discussing the subject "catholicity," Küng states:

> The total Church is the Church as manifested, represented and realized in the local Churches. Inasmuch as the Church in this sense of the *total* Church is the *entire* Church it may be called, according to the original use of the word, the *Catholic*, that is the whole, universal, all-embracing Church. Catholicity is essentially a question of totality. [81]

Evangelical Catholicism in the style of Hans Küng seems to approach evangelical Protestantism. It should not be overlooked, however, that the institutional Church and its ordinances retain for Küng a crucial role in his order of salvation. Küng devotes a special section to the old Catholic axiom: "There is no salvation outside the Church." In connection with this discussion, Küng strongly affirms: "We believe in salvation through Christ in the Church." [82] Furthermore, this Church is, for Küng, best represented by the Roman Catholic Church.

> We cannot simply ignore one curious fact, which needs explaining: the fact that one Church, from the time of Ignatius of Antioch down to the present day, has very consistently retained as part of its title that age-old attribute . . . (of Catholicity). It is true that other Churches have not only wished to be Catholic, but wished to be called Catholic. But they have always found it necessary to add some further definition (Anglo-Catholic, Old Catholic, and so forth) precisely in order to avoid being confused with the one Church which has remained the "Catholic Church." [83]

In discussing the World Council of Churches as an alternative effort for Christian unity, Küng has high praise for its venture to bring churches into living contact with one another. Küng challenges his readers, Catholics as well as Protestants, to give active support to its cause. By its own confession, however, it does not want to be a world or super church but simply to remain a federative council.[84] The Vatican Council, by contrast, approaches more closely the ideal of restoring the universal Church, in Küng's opinion.

To clarify his idea of spiritual union Küng uses the analogy of the mother church. All the Protestant churches are considered daughter churches and even the Orthodox Churches are seen by Küng as a derivation from Catholicism. According to Küng, this analogy may explain why the Roman Catholic Church "is curiously jealous of her daughters . . . that after such a long time apart she still announces that she has 'rights' over them . . . that she finds it so hard to understand why they will have nothing to do with her old faith. . . ." It may also explain why these grown-up daughters find it inconceivable "reentering their mother's womb; the laws of life do not permit such a return." [85] Küng concludes this analogue by remarking how these daughter churches quarrelled among themselves and how, in consequence, the whole family was split up. The implications of this interpretation of history are that no genuine reunification of the Church can be achieved unless the World Council of Churches includes Rome in its concern, or unless Rome includes the non-Roman Catholic churches in its considerations.

The fact of pluriform Christianity is of tragic dimensions for Küng. "The existence of conflicting Churches has done indescribable harm to the credibility of the Church and its message. . . . Innumerable people have been alienated from the Church itself because of these divisions." [86] In this connection, Küng forgets that the New Testament Church showed great variety and it even experienced inflammatory tensions between such dedicated apostles as Peter and Paul. The unity of the early Church allowed for four differing gospels and for different languages of worship and creed, as Küng himself knows very well.[87] Even heresy was accepted as a fact of life for the militant Church. Jesus allows the tares to remain among the wheat until the harvest time. Küng quotes Paul from 1 Corinthians 11:19, which states: "There must be factions ('heresies') among you in order that those who are genuine among you may be recognized." [88] A great number of the martyrs had heretical tendencies, according to Küng. They often were dedicated men and women who exposed certain weaknesses in the Church.[89] The Church Father Augustine confirmed this view by his admonition: "Do not believe, brethren, that heresies are produced by insignificant souls! Only great men have produced heresies." [90]

If Küng allows for heresy within the Church, why not tolerate a variety of churches alongside the Catholic Church? Why not allow the daughter churches to develop their own pattern of worship and faith? Why could not the associational or federative policy be accepted as it is practiced in the World Council of Churches as well as in evangelical councils? If Küng aims for an evangelical Catholicism centered around Christ, the Word, and the ordinances, why still adhere to the Roman temporal and geographical concepts of historical succession? The Scriptures use quite frequently the analogue of the harvest for the realization of the Kingdom. There is no visible connection between one harvest season and the next. There is, however, the continuity of the sower and his seed, which would refer to the living Lord and his Word. Wherever the Word takes root, the Kingdom of God is being manifested and the *ekklesia* takes form. If the two evangelical marks should have priority, as Küng maintains, then the four classical marks of the Church should be reinterpreted accordingly. Christianity is either Christocentric or ecclesiocentric or either evangelical or institutional. Küng's combination of these two alternatives leads to compromise and will confuse the issue.[91]

5. Assessment

In many ways, Küng's 1967 publication on *The Church* plays a key role in understanding his theological identity. His previous publications were more or less implementations of the principles received from Barth, Congar, and Käsemann. In this ecclesiology Küng has come into his own. In a detailed and critical book report, Congar has a listing of Küng's unique contributions, which includes a theology of the charismas, a theology based on historical-critical exegesis, an integration of spirituality and ecclesiology, and a history of the relation of Christians to Jews.[92] Others have commented that Küng offers a constructive though defective basis for an ecumenical ecclesiology.[93] Yves Congar qualified Küng's study as a rejuvenation of Möhler's pneumatological ecclesiology of 1825.[94]

Küng's *The Church* also provides a clue to his later publications with their ensuing conflicts. Küng's ecclesiology evolved as a reaction to the sudden turn of events during the Second Vatican Council with the succession of Pope John XXIII by Pope Paul VI. His prior contact with Käsemann in Tübingen provided Küng with a charismatic approach to the Church that allowed him to downgrade the institutional Church and its hierarchy. His opponents viewed this as a form of biblicism, which did not take into account the whole New Testament and the later historical development.[95] Even Congar asked rhetorically: "My dear Küng, you are very self-confident. Don't you overestimate your high evaluation of your theological charisma?" [96] Rather than portraying the Church in traditional Catholic manner as originating from Christ through his representatives— the popes, their bishops, and the priests—Küng dwelt on with the charismatic people of God and left the ecclesiastical office almost as an afterthought to his study on the Church. The Petrine office received only the last forty-five pages of his book.[97] Küng's publication, *Infallible? An Inquiry*, was a logical next step even if Pope Paul VI would not have provided an occasion with his encyclical, *Humanae Vitae*, on the issue of birth control.[98] The tension between charisma and office plays a major role in Küng's bestseller, *On Being a Christian.* Also his latest major work on the existence of God bears the stamp of reactionism against traditional Catholic faith. Religion has no sacramental or institutional aspects left; the contemporary prophets are the secular ideologues in economy, sociology, and psychology.

V
Conflict with Rome

1. The Occasion

On the day of Pentecost in 1970, the birthday of the Church, Hans Küng wrote the "Candid Preface" to his most controversial book, *Infallible? An Inquiry.*[1] "The renewal of the Catholic Church . . . has come to a standstill,"[2] was his verdict. In spite of numerous constructive changes, two factors had remained the same: the hierarchical power structure and its instrument—the system of canon law. Five years earlier, Küng had addressed bishops and theologians gathered in Rome during the closing weeks of Vatican II.[3] With a sense of satisfaction, he had stated then and at several occasions since that time that "the success of Vatican II was largely due to the constructive cooperation of the bishops with the theologians, who in most cases prepared the good speeches and suggestions of the bishops and worked out the conciliar documents."[4] Now, five years later, Küng had to concede: "The cooperation between bishops and theologians" had come "largely to a standstill."[5] The hierarchy had assumed its preconciliar role of priestly as well as prophetic or theological authority. "The Roman system is the sole absolutionist system that has survived the French Revolution intact . . ."[6] was Küng's cynical remark. For the first time in his publishing career,

Küng defiantly requested no "imprimatur," that is no episcopal authorization for his "inquiry" on the dogma of infallibility.[7] Küng assures the reader of his "candid preface" that he is still a "convinced Catholic theologian," but that this implies for him the right and the duty "to raise a protest . . . against the way in which . . . the people of God are being deprived of the fruits of the Council."[8]

Ever since Vatican II some "Neuralgic points" had remained, namely: the issue of birth control, the question of mixed marriages, the priestly celibacy in the Latin Church, and the reform of the Roman Curia.[9] These issues had been kept from the agenda during Vatican II, and since then the preconciliar positions on these issues had been affirmed by the Curia and the pope.[10] According to Küng, the primary concern of the Curia had been to preserve the status quo of the institutional Church rather than to serve the well-being of its people and mankind in general.[11] Authority rather than service seemed to be the primary motive for the various actions and promulgations since Vatican II.

The most disturbing papal document for Küng was the encyclical, *Humanae Vitae,* which affirmed the traditional Catholic rejection of any form of artificial birth control.[12] It was issued in 1968 without any input from concerned theologians, sociologists, or medical advisors.[13] The destiny of mankind had to take second place to the concerns of institutional self-preservation. According to Küng, the canon lawyers had convinced Pope Paul VI that a radical change in the attitude toward birth control would endanger the dogma of infallibility and thereby weaken the Church's divine mission. Küng, however, was of the opinion that the Church would strengthen its credibility by admitting a change of mind on the issues involved. The alternatives were *consistency of teaching* or *possibility of change;* of these Küng would choose the latter.[14]

By historical circumstance, Küng was confronted with the same obstacle that the Protestants consistently had mentioned in their rejection of Roman Catholicism, namely the issue of papal infallibility. In the preface to Küng's first publication, Karl Barth had warned: "Do not content yourself with the fine beginning you have made . . . It will certainly take quite an effort . . . to make somewhat plausible to us matters like Transubstantiation, the Sacrifice of the Mass, Mary, and the infallible papacy. . . ."[15] Through his dialogue with Barth and other Protestant theologians, Küng had come to

the conclusion that "ultimately, all questions about the concrete orga-
nizational structure of the Church are crystallized in the question
of the *ecclesiastical office.* "[16]

In his succeeding publications, Küng carefully worked out a distinction between papal primacy and papal infallibility. He had attempted
to win Catholics as well as Protestants for the acceptability and
need of an official rather than an infallible spokesman for Christianity.
In his publication introducing the Council and reunion, Küng had
stated confidently: "The Papacy is recognized today by world public
opinion as a moral force, and recent Popes have won the sympathy
even of much of the non-Catholic world." [17]

Already at this initial stage, however, Karl Rahner had been disturbed by Küng's questioning of the concept of papal infallibility.[18]
Nonetheless, Küng had continued to demonstrate that the definition
of papal infallibility concerns only one aspect of his ministry and
of the infallibility of the Church in general.[19] In his study on the
Structures of the Church, on the eve of Vatican II, Küng devoted
more than three times the number of pages to the Petrine office
than to the concept of infallibility.[20] He had hoped that the Vatican
Council would have achieved a strong concept of collegiality and
decentralization, so that in the future the voice of the bishops, the
theologians, and the laity would be heard. Only with a renewal of
this kind would there be any hope for a reconciliation between Rome
and Reformation. The untimely death of Pope John XXIII occasioned
the beginning of an intensifying disenchantment with the Church.
Until finally in the year 1970, the centennial anniversary of Vatican
I, Küng waged a direct attack on the concept of papal infallibility.
"The alarm had to sound in order to wake the sleeping theologians" [21]
and in order to challenge the pope and his cardinals in Rome.

Küng's strategy had to undergo a sudden shift. The attempts to
dialogue and to reconciliation with the Protestants had to be abandoned, now that Küng had entered the esoteric field of inner-Catholic
polemics. Ten years of an intensive schedule of meetings and correspondence and publication followed. Küng's two most voluminous
books, *On Being a Christian* (1974) and *Does God Exist?* (1978),
were written during those hectic years. Almost a thousand pages
of documents were published by sympathizers of Küng [22] and about
two hundred pages were issued by the German Bishops Conference
in defense of their actions against Küng.[23] On 18 December 1979,

the final verdict was presented to Küng. That same day Küng protested against this decision on German television. Defiantly, he stated: "I must say, it's a scandal when a Church, which appeals to Jesus Christ and intends to defend human rights, still conducts inquisition trials in the middle of the 20th century." [24]

Even though the issue of Christology had become an additional point of controversy, the fatal point of conflict was Küng's reinterpretation of the concept and the practice of infallibility.[25] As John Huss and Martin Luther had experienced centuries earlier, the ultimate criterion of heresy had been the contention that the Council and the pope could err. At this point, Küng had to experience the same intransigence, even of his senior colleague, Karl Rahner. During the Christmas season of 1979, frantic efforts were undertaken to rescind the action by the Congregation of the Doctrine of the Faith withdrawing Küng's credentials to teach as a Catholic theologian. Even on Christmas morning, a last effort was made on behalf of Küng by his associate, Hermann Häring,[26] to no avail. By the end of 1979, on 30 December, the removal of Küng's "missio canonica" was confirmed and a decennium of battle had been concluded.[27]

2. Defining Infallibility

The question has been debated intensively by many Catholic theologians [28] as to what Küng exactly had in mind in his use of the concept of infallibility. Luther clearly rejected any form of primacy or authority of the pope and resolutely took refuge in the Scriptures alone. Küng conceded in an interview: "I do not in fact deny each and every form of infallibility or, what strikes me as a better term, indefectibility." [29] Küng wants to reinterpret rather than to reject. Consistent with his Corinthian view of the Church, Küng considers the body of Christ as the locus of apostolic succession as well as of divine guardianship.[30] In the same interview, Küng continued:

> All I am denying is that indefectibility of the Church in the truth is tied to definite propositions or cases. The positive meaning of this is . . . that the Church will be maintained in the truth of the Gospel on the basis of the promise given to it by Christ, not because its leaders or teachers make no mistakes, but despite all the errors of professors of theology, bishops, and possibly even Popes.[31]

In other words, the message and ministry of the Church is initiated from below rather than from above. The spirit of God is with the people of God in the first place and with its leaders only in a derived sense.[32] Leaders can be deceived or can be actively deceiving, but "the Church will not yield to untruth; it is undeceivable. God has promised and granted to it infallibility. Despite its errors and misunderstandings God will preserve it in truth." [33] This was for the German bishops an absolutely untenable position. As Bishop Moser, in an effort of mediation, expressed his concern in his last letter to Küng: "I find it regrettable that you do not speak about the ecumenical councils in the way the bishops do, namely 'as representing the whole episcopate.' Your version is: 'as representing the whole Church.' Thus you embark on an interpretation of the councils which has often been challenged on historical and dogmatic grounds." [34]

Küng's position comes close to Calvin's concept of the perseverance of the saints. Calvin asserted this doctrine in order to proclaim God as the direct author and sustainer of salvation rather than to give credit to the intermediaries of the Church and the sacraments.[35] Küng, however, claims his concept of indefectibility for the Church that is to remain in the truth forever. In this connection, he quotes John 14:16, but does not make any exegetical remark.[36] The passage reads: "I will give you another counselor, to be with you forever, even the Spirit of Truth." The spirit indeed is "full of grace and truth," as the same gospel maintains of the incarnate Christ (1:14). Is the Church, however, also indefectibly truthful? Do these passages really refer to epistemological or doctrinal truth?

Küng clearly relates the Johannine passages to Paul's concept of epistemological knowledge; and he is well aware that Paul speaks of "imperfect knowledge" in 1 Corinthians 13:9. Although Küng does not explain this passage either, he simply follows the Catholic tradition of interpreting the term "imperfect" by the word "incomplete" rather than by the concept "indistinct" or "unclear." Whatever interpretation is given by Küng, John 14:16 certainly is not a strong supportive passage for an indefectible or infallible Church.[37] There is a distinction between Calvin's soteriological concern and Küng's ecclesiological and epistemological concern. Furthermore, the passages mentioned do not really speak to the issue whether the bishops receive their insight from above or from below. Küng's conviction merely results from a logical deduction of his Corinthian charismatic concept of the Church.[38]

The tension concerning the origin of authority either "from above" or "from below" has only found limited expression in Catholic history. The relationship between the pope and the people of God has limited itself to the interactions between the pope and the episcopacy, which represented the corporate interests of the laity only to a limited degree. Even Vatican II has not been able to engage a representation of the church members. The only political polarity over the centuries was created by the tension between the pope and the council of bishops. During the late Middle Ages, this polarity of power was represented by the parties of the Kurialists over against the Conciliarists. According to Küng, this tension was already foreshadowed in the Gospel of Matthew, which in chapter 16 affirms that Peter had been given the power of binding and loosing, while in chapter 18 this power is given to the college of the twelve disciples.[39]

According to Küng, this perennial tension between the primate and the episcopate has manifested itself in the two recent councils, Vatican I and Vatican II.[40] The former was convened by the proud Pius IX who was acclaimed by some of the council fathers as the "vice-god of mankind" or as an "incarnation of the Son of God." [41] During that notorious council of 1870, Pope Pius IX had rejected any claim of the bishops as being "witnesses of tradition." He retorted, "Witnesses of tradition? . . . there is only one; that's me." The popular version of this statement was: "Tradition, that's me!" [42] About ninety years later, a totally opposite attitude was taken by the humble Pope John XXIII. On one occasion, he stated with a smile: "I'm not infallible; I'm infallible only when I speak 'ex cathedra.' But I'll never speak 'ex cathedra'!" [43] The term "ex Cathedra" appears in the 1870 statement of infallibility and indicates the presence of the college of bishops.[44]

The definition of infallibility is evidently dependent upon the perspective of the beholder. If infallibility originates from the pope as representative of Christ, its authority tends to be an absolute power. If, however, the infallible truth resides with the "Body of Christ" then the pope is rather an executive servant of his Church. In other words, the definition of infallibility can be given from a high-church or from a low-church perspective. For Küng, the issue is settled.

Divine guidance and truth is infallibly given to the people, even in spite of the errors of popes and bishops. "The *whole* Church is the temple of the Spirit, built on the foundation of the apostles." [45] "As an individual Christian, I must become a true successor of the apostles; I must hear their witness, believe their message, initiate their mission and ministry." [46]

In his book on the *Structures of the Church,* Küng had already made a strong case for "The Laity in Conciliar History." [47] In that connection, he made a special reference to a laywoman, namely, Empress Irene who presided over the seventh ecumenical council in 787. Consistently, Küng has presented a low-church viewpoint that finally clashed with the traditional concept of papal infallibility.[48] A low-church view would also mean that the bishops could depose a pope, as it actually took place during the Council of Constance.[49] Küng points out that even contemporary canon law lists five criteria for determining the end of papal authority.[50] Three of these are self-evident since they are death, resignation, and mental illness. Two of those criteria, namely, heresy and schism, however, are consistent with the notorious principle of "the Council above the Pope" as it was formulated during the Council of Constance.[51]

The centuries of discussion as well as Küng's own experiences should teach the reader a lesson. If God's work has found a better continuation among the "People of God" than among its leaders, Küng ought to be given credit for affirming the indefectibility of the Church rather than of the pope. History should also teach one, however, that papal primacy cannot be welded to episcopal or congregational authority, as Küng had hoped to achieve. Yves Congar clearly demonstrated the contrast between a hierarchical church and congregational polity in his book, *Divided Christendom.* A conscious choice has to be made between an infallible hierarchical institution or an indefectible congregational movement of Christians.

A Baptist participant, J. W. McClendon, in the dialogue on papal infallibility, generously allowed for a "president of the Christian world community," as he expressed it. The condition was added, however, that this president would be elected for a limited period of time.[52] Such a policy would, indeed, protect the continuity of the Christian churches and would guarantee at the same time a certain discontinuity of top leadership. Most Evangelicals, though, would resist any form of worldwide and centralized leadership for any period of time. The experience of dark and long centuries caused by Roman leadership will discourage such proposals for the next several centuries.

3. The Apostolic Succession

Küng's conflict with Rome came into the open with his questioning of papal infallibility. The same tension was dormant already in his interpretation of the much older Catholic concept of apostolic succession.[53] Just as the term "infallibility" developed in later centuries, so the concept "apostolic succession" is not found in the New Testament.[54] The reference to the function of apostleship is used most frequently by the evangelist, Luke, especially in his book of Acts, and by the apostle, Paul.

According to Küng, the function of apostleship for Paul means first of all to be witnesses of the risen Lord and, secondly, to be commissioned for missionary preaching.[55] On the question, "Who are those commissioned to witness and proclaim?" Küng stated unambiguously: "The whole Church, not just a few individuals . . . is the successor of the apostles in obedience, and from this obedience it derives its authority." [56] Every individual Christian is challenged to follow the mission and service of the original twelve apostles. By this interpretation, Küng has changed the concept of apostolic succession from a principle of church order to a concept of ministry for all believers.

The dogma of apostolic succession has been the oldest argument for Roman primacy and authority in the Christian world. Apostolic succession has always meant Petrinic succession by the bishop of Rome. The traditional Scripture passage was Matthew 16:18: "And I tell you, you are Peter, and on this rock I will build my church . . . I will give you the keys of the kingdom of heaven. . . ." Hans Küng did not hesitate to attack even this most sacred argument of his Church. Küng demonstrates from the first epistle of Clement and from Ignatius, both second century documents, that there was no monarchical bishop at Rome during that time.[57] The particular Roman interpretation of Matthew 16:18 is first used by Tertullian at the end of the second century.[58]

The rejection of the traditional Roman Catholic interpretation of the apostolic succession should not be confused with the concept

of Roman primacy. Küng is strongly convinced of the eminence of
the Roman Church from the very earliest beginnings of Christianity.
The primacy of Rome was, however, a mere matter of historical
circumstance rather than an apostolic bestowal of universal authority.[59] For Küng, as for the Anglicans and the Orthodox churches,
apostolic succession refers to all Christians who follow the apostolic
word of the Scriptures.

In discussing the concept of apostolic succession, Küng follows
the same procedure as in his definition of infallibility. In both instances, he creates a distance between the primacy of Rome and
the general Christian qualities of infallibility and apostolic succession.
In both cases, he recommends a synonym for the sake of reinterpretation. The dogma of papal infallibility is replaced by ecclesiastical
indefectibility, while the dogma of apostolic succession is reformu-
lated as "perpetuity" or "indestructibility." [60] The Church as a whole
in its failures and victories reflects the apostolic model. Also the
apostle, Peter, had his defeats. Küng gives a brief exposition of
the three basic Scripture references to Peter that demonstrate how
each moment of leadership is followed by an evidence of his
weakness.[61] So, the Church is a community of sinners as well as a
community of saints. "The Church may forsake her God; he will
not forsake her." [62] It may have its disastrous eras, but it will not
be overcome by the powers of darkness. "Succeeding the apostles"
means for Küng not a divine authorization for the Roman Church
leadership, but rather a historical evidence of salvation history. As
an evangelical Catholic, Hans Küng can write about his Church in
ebullient terms:

> God will ensure that there will always be a Church and that it
> will be holy . . . Though wounded it will remain alive, though sinning
> it will not fall away from grace, though erring it will never lose
> sight of the truth . . . As the Fathers explained, it can become a
> beggar woman, set itself up as a trader, sell itself as a prostitute;
> but through God's preserving, saving and forgiving mercy it will
> always remain the bride of Christ.[63]

It is strange that Küng considers himself a genuine disciple of
Yves Congar in his concept of a general apostolic succession of
the Church. In a public response to Congar's critique, Küng stated:

"Congar has been my major model for Catholic theology . . . In spite of all differences I am his son in the area of ecclesiology." [64] Congar does, indeed, accept a general apostolic succession, but very emphatically he adds to this the "direct and original succession of officers through Christ in the apostles. . . ." [65] The Congregation of Faith of the Vatican in its official rejection of both Küng's books, *The Church* and *Infallible? An Inquiry* hesitates to speak of a general apostolic succession. It does accept the concept of the priesthood of all believers, but reserves the concept of apostolic succession for bishops and priests. It affirms that "Christ, the head of the Church, which is his mystical body, has ordained his apostles as servants of his priesthood." [66] It reminds the readers that these officers have received the seal of Christ by their ordination, so that the clergy possesses a special place of responsibility.

Even though the conflict on the issue of infallibility was more flagrant and sensational, the issue of apostolic succession struck more at the heart of the Vatican leadership. On the basis of the Scripture, Küng maintains, however, that there is no trace of a direct commission of the bishops by Christ. Christ sent his disciples into the world and, after several generations of complex historical development, the episcopate came into being. Küng remarks: "This is perhaps the only point where I find myself interpreted incorrectly by Congar. I am not reducing the total 'apostolic succession' to the apostolate of the Church, even though the apostolic service of the total Church and of every individual member seems basic to me." [67]

It is hard to imagine how Küng could consider his proposal of an original general apostolate acceptable to Catholic theology and leadership. Ever since the second century of the Christian era, the role of the bishop, together with the canon and the creed, was considered a stronghold against heresy and schism. Can one consider oneself a genuine Catholic while playing down the role of bishops and popes? Among the many Catholic leaders commenting on Küng's principles none has endorsed his general apostolate. [68] Only Protestants praised his "consistent dialectic of charisma and office," and his "proximity to the Reformers." [69] There was, indeed, a declaration by 1360 Catholic theologians arguing for the freedom of theology. [70] This gesture of adhesion, however, did not mention any particular theological issue. The Catholic Church would lose its identity without its traditional concept of apostolic succession. It might have been better for Küng to reject this concept outright rather than redefining a historical and sacred tradition of his Church.

If Küng, indeed, intended to return to the earliest levels of the Christian community, he would simply find the commission by Christ to his followers to go out into the world teaching, baptizing, and observing all that had been commanded to them (Matthew 28:19–20). This mission includes, however, no directives for a charismatic or episcopal church order. Under the guidance of the Holy Spirit, a variety of church organizations developed already before the close of the New Testament canon. The episcopal model seems to have been the answer for the unstable situation of the early Christian era. Since the Reformation, the presbyterian and the congregational model developed in reaction to episcopal failure and in harmony with a greater congregational maturity. Why not simply accept the development of the history of salvation rather than "recycle" traditional concepts? After all, the term "apostolic succession" is not part of the New Testament text. Evangelical Protestants would welcome Küng's spirit of renewal, but they would more openly reject those developments in Christianity which either have served their time or were ostensibly wrong.

4. The Ministry of the Word

A third major area of conflict centers in Küng's own identity as a theologian. One of his formative life's experiences was the participation in Vatican II as a "peritus," as a qualified theologian.[71] As was mentioned above,[72] Küng considered the cooperation of theologians and bishops *the* unique feature of the Vatican conference. In his *Structures of the Church,* Küng had demonstrated already before the Vatican sessions how the early Church allowed a greater place of responsibility to the theologian and how the disastrous Vatican I by contrast had been almost devoid of theological assistance.[73] In his publications since Vatican II, Küng deplored the return of the authoritative magisterium [74] and blames the cessation of further development of the Church on the increasing avoidance of theological advice by the Vatican leaders.[75]

In his biblical reorientation, Küng identified the theologian with the Old Testament prophets. The tension between Jesus and the priests in the New Testament is projected into Küng's contemporary conflict with the Vatican and the German Conference of Bishops.[76] Since theologians in the early Christian era were mostly laymen, Küng alternately argued for the charisma of the theologian and of the layman. Both of these find their identity in the ministry of the Word in contrast to the church leaders who basically are involved in the exercise of power, according to Küng.

One of the contested [77] distinctions that Küng makes is the difference between the New Testament concepts of authority (*exousia*) and service (*diakonia*).[78] Pope John XXIII embodied the servant role beautifully. On the day of his election, he asked for God's blessing on his "very humble office of shepherd" and, in his coronation mass, he introduced himself with the words: "I am Joseph, your brother." [79] For Küng, this humble pope was one of the very few, if not the only pope, who understood the ministry of service. Here was the apostolic spirit that Luther missed among the hierarchs of his day.[80] On the basis of the Corinthian model of the Church, every member of the Church, male as well as female, can be involved in the ministry of service. Therefore, "the whole fellowship of Jesus' disciples considers itself empowered to forgive sins, as also to administer baptism and so celebrate the Lord's Supper, since the Spirit has been given to it as a whole." [81] Even though Küng merely describes a New Testament situation, it is obvious that he recommends a shift to a more congregational pattern of ministry. Also, the Congregation of the Faith in Rome understood Küng's suggestive statements in this manner:

> The testimony of the ecclesiastical tradition and of the ecclesiastical teaching office are agreed, that the believers who have not received the priestly ordination and who yet presumptuously celebrate the eucharist, are performing this without permission and without validity. It is evident that such abuses when they occur should be discontinued by the Shepherd of the Church.[82]

After having discussed the role of the theologian and the layperson in ministry, Küng tackles the popular concept of "the priesthood of all believers" derived from 1 Peter 2:9.[83] These words cannot be used to endorse the Catholic concept of the priesthood and its sacramental ministry. The apostle Peter rather claims the purpose of proclamation in connection with the symbol "priesthood" used for the Christian community.[84] Küng agrees with Luther who used this verse as the principle of Protestantism, which involved each member of the congregation. Returning to the New Testament for his orientation, Küng demonstrates that the term "priest" is not used once in all of the New Testament for someone holding an office in the church. Also, Jesus in his preaching "takes his images not from the priestly ministry but from the secular world around him." [85]

Although the first disciples saw Jesus as one of the prophets (Matthew 16:14), the first Christian congregations began to see in Jesus the great high priest (Hebrews 5:10). After a detailed exposé of the relevant verses in the book of Hebrews, Küng concludes that the death of Jesus does not introduce but rather supersedes the traditional priesthood.[86] The prophetic ministry of the Word is the typical characteristic of early Christianity. When Peter used the symbol of the priesthood for each Christian, he intended to indicate that every believer has direct access to God. The book of Hebrews confirms that "all are washed with pure water, in order to draw near to God" (Hebrews 10:22).[87] Küng remarks with regret: "We are forced to conclude that the originally rich idea of the priesthood of all believers was largely lost during centuries of clericalization and only gradually regained in very recent times." [88]

For Evangelical Protestants, it is refreshing to read Küng's plea for the renewal of lay preaching. Even though he is no specialist in the great variety of lay movements, Küng asserts that lay preaching was practiced by men and women through all of the Christian era. The Reformation caused a bifurcation in the practice of lay preaching. While the Protestant movement achieved a great increase in lay preaching and lay theology, the Catholic leadership withdrew itself to the territory of ordained clergy. "The Council of Trent decided that sermons in the strict sense should be reserved for bishops and their assistants." [89] Preaching was increasingly neglected until the Codex of Canon Law in 1918 proclaimed a general ban on lay preaching.[90]

Lay theology had a greater chance of survival. Among a considerable list of Catholic scholars, Küng mentions Blaise Pascal.[91] Küng never fails to mention the need for the involvement of laywomen. "From a theological viewpoint there is not the slightest reason why lay theologians of either sex who have doctorates in theology should not be allowed to teach in faculties of theology." [92] Küng wants the Roman Catholic Church to return to a serious theological concern. "A Church in which theologians have to keep silent becomes an untruthful Church." [93] Theology has great potential for determining the future direction of the Church. Theology "employs all the means of research and scholarship to reflect anew on the original message, theology is able of finding old keys which the Church has mislaid. . . ." [94]

Küng's desire to return to the Corinthian model of the Church is somewhat in conflict with his earlier statements during the fall of 1962 concerning the presence of early Catholicism in the New Testament.[95] At that time, he strongly argued for a charismatic church plus an institutional one, for a church having its roots in Corinth as well as in Jerusalem. Since his disenchantment with the Vatican leadership after the death of Pope John XXIII in 1963, Küng increasingly talks about the fatal process of "clericalization," which has dimmed the original spirituality of the New Testament Church.[96] Küng continues to believe in the need for ordained leadership, but the process of clericalization is for him a search for authority replacing a life of service.[97] The process of deterioration set in as soon as the nomenclature "priest" was applied to the leader of the congregation. Even though the term priest is linguistically derived from the Greek word "presbuteros" (elder), its content was increasingly influenced by the pagan priesthood.[98] The celebration of the eschatological meal became a solemn sacrifice; the priesthood of all believers was soon dissolved in the fatal separation of clergy and laity.[99] The clergy soon developed into a hierarchy with the bishop as its absolute monarch. These princes of the Church were adorned with distinctive attributes as time progressed. Finally, the "apostolic succession" became a juridical claim by a metropolitan bishop replacing the original apostolic service and witness of all believers by monarchical authority.

At present, "a frightening gulf separates the Church of today from the original constitution of the Church." [100] Küng expresses a certain jealousy of the Free Churches who "seem to have more impetus than well-ordered Churches with a complete hierarchy." [101] Küng wants to maintain, however, a dialectic tension between char-

isma and office, between spontaneous service and appointed leadership. He seems to mute his virile argument for spiritual spontaneity
by concluding:

> All Christians have authority to preach the word . . . but only
> pastors with a special calling . . . have the particular authority to
> preach in the meetings of the community. . . . All Christians are
> empowered to share in the celebrations of baptism and the Lord's
> Supper. But only pastors with a special calling have the particular
> authority to administer baptism in the public assembly . . . and to
> be responsible for leading the celebration of the Lord's Supper in
> the community.[102]

What then remains of the general indefectibility, the general apostolic succession, and the general ministry of the Word, if only the
ordained leaders can qualify for the particular acts of ministry?
Why is the Vatican leadership disturbed if the whole discussion is
a matter of mere words?

5. Reaction and Response

The publication of *Infallible? An Inquiry* drew a wide response
from the media and the public. The Vatican, which apparently attempted to ignore as much as possible Küng's regular publications
and speeches, finally had to take some action. No final evaluation
of Küng's book, *The Church* (1967), had been formulated yet. Acci-
dentally, an informal listing of remarks on this particular book by
the Congregation of the Faith came into Küng's hands.[103] An intense
series of letters was written in Tübingen and Rome during the period
1970 until 1975.[104]

A crucial document in this timespan was the official declaration
by the Congregation of the Faith on all of Küng's publications on
the Church issued on 5 July 1973. Its initial words gave the title
to this decisive statement called "Mysterium Ecclesiae." [105] After
affirming the traditional Catholic interpretations, the document explicitly rejects Küng's claim to a certain prophetic stance towards the
Church. "The valid freedom of theologians must remain within the
boundaries given by the Word of God, as the Church has faithfully
preserved and declared this and as it is taught and expounded by

the living teaching office of the shepherds, especially by the shepherd of the total people of God." [106]

Küng was invited to appear in Rome to give account of his continuing rejection of Rome's traditional interpretations. Since several Catholic leaders had been treated unjustly [107] in the years since Vatican II, Küng wanted to ensure a fair hearing. Two extensive letters were written to the Congregation of the Faith on 24 January 1972 and on 22 September 1973.[108] Küng set forth his objections against the traditional proceedings of the Congregation led by the aged Franjo Cardinal Šeper and requested access to the secret file set up on his case ever since his first publication, *Justification, The Doctrine of Karl Barth.* As Küng mentioned in one of his letters: "In all civilized countries of Western Europe even criminals have the right of complete access to the files on their case." [109] In spite of or maybe because of this elaborate correspondence, it never came to a hearing. In frustration, Küng wrote a letter to Pope Paul VI in person stating: "I expect basically nothing more nor anything less than being allowed to study and to teach without being brought under suspicion . . . I do not need to be vindicated. The truth must come to light, nothing more and nothing less . . . I know that one word by you, Holiness, will suffice to bring this case on the right track." [110]

Two letters in a more conciliatory tone by the Congregation brought this discussion to a conclusion.[111] The procedures are explained and the responsibility of theologians was recognized. Reference is made to the request by Pope Paul VI not to teach or write on the controversial subjects until further light was received.[112] Four years later, in the year 1979, Küng could not resist the urge to write a preface to A. B. Hasler's book, *How the Pope Became Infallible.* [113] Within a year's time, the Vatican dealt with his case under the decisive leadership of Pope John Paul II, and Küng lost his "missio canonica." Since December 1979, Küng is not allowed anymore to teach ministerial students seeking ordination in the Roman Catholic Church.

In the meantime, he has shifted the focus of this attention. In an interview during the year of his latest major book, *Does God Exist?* (1978), Küng made the following statements:

> I have in a new fashion become involved in the questions of my contemporaries, including those outside Church institutions . . . I

have honestly had enough of continually defending myself against bishops and their tame theologians . . . What honestly fascinates me is everything that is of significance for us theologians today in astrophysics, in atomic theory, in microbiology, in psychoanalysis, in philosophy and scientific theory—but also in literature, art and music.[114]

Küng has taken off from the launching pad of inner church deliberations and found himself in the wide world of human concerns. Pope John XXIII had laid the groundwork for this expansion, too. His "Message to Humanity" had challenged Christians and all men of good will to cooperate in the building of "a more just and brotherly city in this world." [115] The pope's prayer at that time was providential: "Our prayer is that in the midst of this world there may radiate the light of our great hope in Jesus Christ, our only Savior." [116] At this juncture in his life, Küng demonstrated that he was ready to implement that vision.

VI
On Being a Christian

1. Approach and Presuppositions

Hardly had the publication on the question of infallibility reached its readers during the summer of 1970 when Küng was again involved in a new subject. During the month of September of that same year Küng delivered an address at a world congress of Catholic theologians in Brussels.[1] His subject was: "What is the Christian Message?" This address became a synopsis of Küng's following and most popular book, *On Being a Christian,* published in 1974.[2] In both instances Küng presented the person of Jesus Christ as *the* program of the Christian faith. According to Küng, Jesus was unique in the fact that he identified himself neither with the left nor with the right, neither with the rebels nor with establishment.

Küng challenges his readers primarily to a commitment to the living Christ and only belatedly to a dedication to the institutional Church. The leaders of the Church, particularly of the Roman Catholic Church, are compared with the opponents of the historical Jesus: the Sadducees, the Zealots, the Essenes, and the Pharisees. It seems contradictory when Küng contends this book to be a positive counterpart to his polemics on the issue of infallibility.[3] Its message, indeed, is positive, namely for the individual believer and for the world at large. There is, however, no positive note for any established church, unless it is overruled by the victory of Jesus Christ who "constantly proves to be stronger than all human incapacity and superficiality." [4] It is no wonder that Küng again kindled the ire of his superiors. We find it hard to believe that Küng himself was genuinely amazed about the response he evoked among the leadership of his Church.[5]

Küng qualifies his work as "a small summa" [6] indicating a comprehensive doctrinal statement. That his study leaves out essential components of the Christian faith, however, he is well aware. He apologizes, for instance, that he omitted discussions on prayer, on meditation, and on worship, supposedly because of a tight schedule.[7] Several reviewers express regret about such inappropriate haste, but none of them associates this oversight with Küng's one-sided attempt to extol Christ's role in society and in personal life at the expense of the church. For the Roman Catholic believer the subject of worship is related to the church as the mediatrix of salvation, which is constituted upon the seven sacraments which as channels of grace provide eternal sanctification.

Küng chooses in a Protestant manner to focus on the living Mediator Jesus Christ rather than on the sacred mediation of the Roman Catholic Church. In quite evangelical fashion only two questions guide Küng's thought throughout this book: "Who is Christ?" and "What does it mean to be a Christian?" Küng's book was hailed by Avery Dulles as "a highly effective apologia for basic Christianity." [8] Assuming this evaluation is correct the emphasis of this statement should be on the basic rather than on the apologetic-quality of Küng's book. Küng, indeed, wants to deal in a pastoral manner with the common man's faith instead of providing an academic apologetic for his church.

In agreement with this stance Hans Küng addresses his work to those "who do not believe, but nevertheless seriously inquire; who did believe, but are not satisfied with their unbelief; who do believe, but feel insecure in their faith." [9] By these categories Küng refers first of all to the disenchanted Neo-Marxists among whom he detects an increasing concern for the ultimate issues of life, for the questions of suffering and death, of justice and love. In the light of such questions the progressive Marxists have, indeed, discovered the potential significance of religion.[10] In his subsequent book on the reality of God Küng will give ample attention to the atheist and the secularist.

In the book under discussion Küng concentrates, however, on the second group which once did believe and is at present a victim of doubt and unbelief. This group includes the thousands of lay persons and clergymen who have abandoned their places in the increasingly deserted churches. It is for the benefit of these people that Küng wants to provide a believable faith. Küng shows himself to be more concerned with the seekers than with those "who believe, but feel insecure in their faith." He will deal with this group in his third doctrinal study on *Eternal Life.* [11] Finally Küng expresses the intention to enter into dialogue with the world's living religions: "We need an *oikoumene . . .* no longer based on missionary conquest of the other religions, but listening to their concerns, sharing their needs and at the same time giving a living testimony of its own faith in word and deed." [12] Küng may follow this direction in future years; in his present publication he only briefly discusses other religions. In our presentation we will follow Küng's major emphasis in his book, *On Being a Christian,* namely his attempt to reason with the disenchanted Christian.

Küng's trilogy: on the Christian life, on the existence of God and on eternal life, is undergirded by Erikson's thesis that a healthy personality needs a "basic trust" in other human beings as well as in life in general.[13] Erikson demonstrates that this basic trust is gained from the first year of man's life and thus controls all of life's events.[14] Conversely, "basic mistrust" is a lifelong counterpoint causing estrangement, neuroses and ultimately self-destruction. Repeatedly Küng expresses his conviction that being a Christian fulfills this existential need of basic trust. In Christ man feels secure in relation to society, his fellow man, and ultimately to the whole of creation. Using the terminology of Paul Tillich, Küng defines religion in general as *"a particular social realization of a relationship to an absolute ground of meaning."* [15] Such a relational religion must become an attitude of life rather than a mere dogmatic acceptance of the great creeds of Christianity; a basic trust should pervade all life situations rather than remain localized in limited sacramental occasions.

Such a relational faith should be tested, however, against the norms of common sense and especially against the Scriptures. Man's faith should neither be purely subjective or fideistic in a Barthian sense nor strongly objectivistic or rationalistic in a Thomistic sense.[16]

Faith should be a merger of personal trust and objective rational evidence. Küng wants, therefore, to complement Erikson's psychological insight with logical philosophical evidence. Erikson should be integrated into a Kantian or Hegelian frame of reference. Küng endorses the contemporary philosopher, William Stegmüller, when he describes faith as "a rationally justifiable fundamental trust." [17] Consequently, Küng continually introduces his Christian affirmations with conditional phrases similar to Pascal's wager argument. In connection with the reality of God Küng states for instance: "If God existed, then a fundamental solution *would be* provided of the enigma of permanently uncertain reality . . . If! But from the hypothesis of God we cannot conclude to the reality of God." [18] Faith in God is not a matter of logical argument but it certainly is the most reasonable option for a basic trust. For this reason Küng rejects rationalistic beliefs as well as blind faith and opts instead for a rationally justifiable basic trust.

Such a merger of existential trust and reasonable evidence requires a definite methodological procedure. Küng discovered this dialectic of subjective ideas verified by objective evidence in Hegel's phenomenology. Ever since his student years in Rome Küng has cultivated an interest in the methodology of this famous German philosopher. By 1970 Küng had completed a minutely researched chronological development of Hegel's thought. This study was published at the occasion of the bicentennial celebration of Hegel's birth.[19] This interest in Hegel formed another major influence on Küng's publications of the seventies. Also Hegel focused on Christ as the synthesis between subjective faith and objective reason; he too points to the resurrection of Christ as the tangent between time and eternity; and, finally also, Hegel had already defined faith as a reasonable trust.[20]

The characteristic Hegelian concept which also Küng frequently uses is the term "sublation." It means "cancelling" as well as "preserving." [21] Thus when two polarities are confronted with one another, their weaknesses are cancelled out while their strengths are preserved in their synthesis. This means concretely for Küng, for instance, that the antithesis Catholicism and Protestantism will be resolved in a higher form of Christianity. A similar "sublation" can be applied to the tension of economic systems like Capitalism and Marxism or to cultural patterns like individualism and totalitarianism. This Hegelian method requires a consistent questioning of past and present positions, because the "sublation" or the ideal is always a step ahead. Applied to the Christian religion, this procedure yields a progressive stance accepting tradition and past forms only as far as they serve the future realization of the kingdom of God. Consequently Küng does not want to be a staunch conservatist preserving merely historical insights, nor does he intend to be a radical innovator advocating daring formulations and novel forms of Christianity. Küng does want to reach out for new manifestations of the kingdom of God as they emerge dialectically from the history of Christianity.[22]

Summarizing this analysis of Küng's approach and presuppositions, we should point out that his procedure results in a blending of a host of voices into one message to contemporary man. Among these voices still remains Käsemann's emphasis on early charismatic Christianity; the style of argument is Hegel's dialectic method embracing time and eternity within the Word incarnate; the pragmatic application of these ideas is couched in the practical reason of Pascal and Kant merging intuition or conscience with rational evidence; the pastoral relevance of Küng's message is found in Erikson's psychological analysis of man's primal need of basic trust; the counterpoint remains Barth's stance of authoritative revelation given to each person who is justified by grace. A great number of supportive recent voices are integrated to demonstrate the progressing reality of the kingdom of God.

In evaluating Küng Catholic scholars have missed an adequate reference to their authoritative dogmatic tradition; [23] they also have difficulty with his Barthian stance making the living Christ experienced by the individual the criterion for past and future.[24] Many reviewers have, indeed, mentioned Küng's perspicuity and confident courage. English-speaking evangelical readers will have difficulty with the German philosophical frame of reference resulting from the blending of these particular voices.

2. The Historical Christ As Model

The main thesis of Küng's bestseller is: being a Christian means to follow Christ. This thesis is simple enough, but Küng needs almost 700 pages to explain the implications of his axiom. Being a Christian means more than being involved in a meditation- or an action-group;

practicing a Christian lifestyle or having theological convictions does
not necessarily point to a Christ-related life either.[25] According to
Küng, "the most fundamental characteristic of Christianity is that
it considers this Jesus as ultimately decisive, definitive, *archetypal*
for man in the various dimensions" of life.[26] A genuine Christian
should be a follower of the Jesus of history. "The kerygma of the
community simply cannot be understood unless we begin quite concretely with the historical Jesus of Nazareth." [27]

Contemporary authors like Erich Kästner and Ernest Hemingway
have called attention to the historical Jesus by stressing his
humanity.[28] The pop-music by the ex-Beatle, George Harrison, expressed this emphasis in the words: "My sweet Lord, I really want
to know you." [29] According to Küng these authors see Jesus "as
the victim abused by everyone, as the most constant and most available symbol for purity, joy, final surrender, and true life." [30] If poets,
writers and musicians are so perceptive to human need in their
focusing on the man Jesus how much more should the theologian
be accountable to his community in portraying Jesus as he spoke
and served in the humble surroundings of Palestine? [31] Too often
the dogmaticians have presented a "plaster Christ . . . who neither
feels nor can feel pain." [32]

The return to the historical Jesus is a direct application of Küng's
design to present faith within a scholarly, justifiable context. The
Church and its members cannot ignore three hundred years of concentrated effort in historical criticism, according to Küng.[33] The Bible
has become the most intensely investigated and the most widely
translated book. Küng refers to the helpful contributions of textual
and literary criticism and to the insight gained by form criticism.
The history of tradition research has even included the pre-literary
conditions in its study of the biblical text. All these resources have
become available to the theologian and indirectly to church members.

Can one be blessed or even be saved without this historical insight?
Küng would definitely answer this in the affirmative.[34] If a choice
had to be made between an "unhistorical faith" and a purely "historical faith" the former would deserve preference. Küng does take
the liberty, however, to qualify this unhistorical faith as a "naive
faith" and warns that such faith could become perilous. Only a
blending of faith and knowledge can provide the mature insight
needed for being a Christian in our modern era.

A historical approach to faith and its proclamation also means assigning a secondary role to exclusively transcendental images of Christ. Küng does not get tired in pointing out that the theologian should begin "from below," from the historical Jesus, rather than "from above," namely from the pre-existent logos, as his seniors Hegel and Barth had done.[35] Also the classic Christian creeds are criticized for having fostered an emphasis on the divine nature of Christ at the expense of his humanity.[36] Those early creeds had the historical function of defending the Christian faith in confrontation with a host of emerging heresies impairing the divine identity of Jesus Christ. For contemporary man, however, the Greek concept of the two natures of Christ has lost its relevance, according to Küng. The classic creeds can even have negative connotations as Küng asserts in his section on "Christ as Dogma":

> Only too often behind the Christ image of the councils there can be perceived the unmoving, passionless countenance of Plato's God, who cannot suffer, embellished with some features of Stoic ethics. . . . But Christ was not born in Greece. . . . The whole doctrine of the two natures is an interpretation in Hellenistic language. . . . What is a Jew, a Chinese, a Japanese or an African, or even the average European or American today, to make of those Greek ciphers? [37]

Küng's reasoning at this point has been quoted somewhat extensively since he has been severely criticized for slighting or even rejecting the divine sonship of Christ.[38] It should be pointed out that Küng does not simply want to reject the early creeds, but that he intends to balance the image of the divine Christ with the traits of the human Jesus for the benefit of the proclamation to contemporary man.[39]

Focusing on the historical Jesus is essential to Küng because he has discovered striking sociological parallels between the story of Jesus and contemporary life situations. Jesus experienced conflicts similar to those of twentieth-century man. Because of his own ecclesiastical confrontations Hans Küng identifies with Jesus in his conflict with the "establishment," to use a term which became current during the turbulent sixties.[40] The ruling class in the New Testament era was the hierarchy of Jewish priests who controlled worship in the temple and politics in the house of the Sanhedrin.

Küng demonstrates the parallels between the Sadducees in Jesus' day and the power struggle of Catholic hierarchs in this century. In both cases these leaders are "outwardly progressive, in regard to others; conservative to reactionary within their own sphere." [41] The progressiveness of the Sadducees consisted in their support of the Roman sovereignty. They gave this only to maintain their own conservative institutional power. By way of contrast Küng states emphatically that "the Jesus of history was not a member or a sympathizer of the liberal-conservative government party." [42] Jesus was far from being a priest; he was neither ordained nor did he have any aspirations to exercise institutional control. He was foremost a teacher who in the style of the prophets taught about new life, love, joy and peace with God. Jesus was one with the people and made use "of universally intelligible, catchy sayings, short stories, parables, drawn from the plain facts of ordinary life, familiar to everyone." [43]

The religion of the establishment provoked a "theology of revolution," in Jesus' day as well as in recent decennia.[44] If Jesus did not associate with the right he neither lined up with the left, with the revolutionaries or "the Zealots," as they were called in his day.[45] Even though Küng sympathizes with those who critically evaluate social structures he does not endorse any form of political revolution.[46] Also at this point he calls upon the historical Jesus as the criterion for a present-day political stance. Küng must concede to the Manchester theologian, S. G. F. Brandon,[47] that Jesus had at least some associations with the radicals of his day. One of Jesus' followers was called "Simon the Zealot"; the betrayer, Judas Iscariot, may have been related to the same revolutionaries, and so also the brothers John and James who were nicknamed "sons of thunder." It cannot be denied that during the court proceedings Jesus was also suspected of revolutionary motives and accordingly presented by the Roman soldiers as "King of the Jews." "Nevertheless," Küng concludes, "we cannot make Jesus a guerrilla fighter, a rebel, a political agitator and revolutionary or turn his message of God's kingdom into a program of politico-social action. . . ." [48] In his Sermon on the Mount Jesus challenged the crowds "not to resist the evildoer, to do good to those who hate us, to bless those who curse us, to pray for those who persecute us." [49] Küng observes rightly that "Che Guevara (the Cuban guerrilla fighter) . . . or Camillo Torres (the Colombian revolutionary priest) have less right than

Gandhi or Martin Luther King to claim Jesus as their example." [50]

There is a third sociological option which over the centuries has been followed in a great variety of forms, namely the lifestyle of withdrawal, renunciation or "emigration," as Küng calls it. [51] The discovery of the Qumran scrolls in the year 1947 provided graphic detail about communal life during the period immediately preceding Jesus' ministry.[52] John the Baptist showed some similarities to the cultic and ethic habits of this movement; also he performed his ministry in the desert; he too performed the ordinance of baptism and he too had ascetic practices. Through John the Baptist Jesus could be linked to the monks and hermits of his day. These men were called Essenes by Josephus and Philo. Küng agrees that Jesus, indeed, showed some ascetic traits; he left his native region and separated himself from his family; he lived like the medieval mendicants depending on daily support by wealthy friends and dedicated women. Jesus also led a celibate life and challenged his disciples to leave their business and family life behind.

Küng demonstrates how Jesus did not withdraw from society and how his first miracle was performed at a wedding feast. Jesus did not require a monastic habit to indicate separation from the world; he did not institute communities nor did he formulate rules or require vows; no ascetic or devotional exercises were prescribed to his disciples. In spite of all these facts Jesus has been claimed in recent decennia by "Jesus-freaks" and "hippies." Charles Reich predicted in his bestseller, *The Greening of America*, a general withdrawal from the economic-political scene into a life of inner peace, love and joy of life as a result of these antiestablishment movements.[53] Küng meets the new breed of the sixties and seventies with understanding and has a genuine appreciation for the great achievements of monasticism.[54] His "fatherly friend," Yves Congar, was a Dominican priest. Yet, Küng quite resolutely states that all these movements "could appeal to the example of the monastic community of Qumran. But they could scarcely claim Jesus as a model." [55]

Küng identifies yet another direction in the sociology of the New Testament, namely the party of the Pharisees who represented still another form of withdrawal from society. As those engaged in politics were either belonging to the right or to the left, so did those who were withdrawing from political life. The radical Essenes could be considered leftists in comparison with the pious Pharisees. Both parties hoped for an overthrow of the Roman authorities not by their own scheming but through the coming of the Messiah.[56]

According to Küng, both parties emerged from the Maccabean movement. They were divided in reaction to the bloody encounter of the Maccabean priest-king, Alexander Jannäus (176–103 B.C.) with the Romans. Since that time the Pharisees were strictly pacifist. Unlike the militant Essenes they aspired preparing the way for the Messiah by study, prayer and strict observation of the Law.[57] Their name may have been derived from the Aramaic word *perishaiia* meaning "the separated ones." They avoided any form of relationship with gentiles and public sinners and were guiding the people in the study of the Law of Moses. They also developed an oral tradition concerning specific applications of the Law, which sometimes led to absurd cases. Küng uses the term "compromise" for the social role of the Pharisees.[58] He describes their stance as an attitude of "ambiguity, duplicity, two-facedness, half measures: tactical maneuvering between the established order and the radicalisms, abandoning any attempt . . . to shape life according to *one* standard. . . ." [59]

Because Jesus was close to the *concerns* of the Pharisees his conflict with them was all the more vehement. Also Jesus was seeking the fulfillment of the Law but he stressed inner motivation where they emphasized external behavior. Jesus also attended the synagogue but he did not agree with their concern for rituals, the accumulation of good works and their moral casuistry. Küng points out that the Pharisees actually devised a merit system similar to the penitential practices of the medieval Catholic Church.[60] He devotes several pages to the psychological comfort such a legalistic system provides to its adherents.

As the Pharisees have undermined religious Judaism so the "court theologians" or the canon lawyers have caused a similar hypocrisy in the Roman Catholic Church. In earlier publications Küng pointed to the ghetto mentality resulting from this isolationist stance among Jews as well as among post-Reformation Roman Catholicism. Thus Pharisaism and ecclesiastical theologians separated their followers increasingly from the mainstream of public life.[61] Küng does not discuss to what degree this a-political stance has caused the impoverishment of Latin America. Many Catholic leaders in that continent have, indeed, called for a change from sacred withdrawal to a theology of liberation or even of revolution. Küng likes to reminisce about the great days of Vatican II when a real open stance toward the world seemed imminent. At the writing of his book *On Being a Christian* he, however, exclaims in resignation:

> In the great conflict Rome was the military victor. Zealotism broke down, Essenism was eradicated, Sadduceeism left without temple or temple ministry. But Pharisaism survived the catastrophe of the year 70. Only the scribes remained as leaders of the enslaved people. . . . But Pharisaism lives on also—and sometimes more so—in Christianity. But it is contrary to the spirit of Jesus himself.[62]

Thus Küng has carefully developed a "quadrilateral" response to the Jesus of history. He locates each of these options in contemporary religion and especially in his own Roman Catholic Church.[63] The Sadducees representing the establishment are the bishops in their various ranks; the Zealots are the Catholic and Protestant Liberation theologians; the ascetic Essenes represent the monastic movement and similar non-Catholic withdrawal movements; the Pharisees, finally, are the canon lawyers of past and present leading the common faithful to a life of legalistic observance. Küng challenges his readers to identify with Jesus who stood far above those social options. Following Jesus in this context means an attitude critical toward the ruling forces of traditional Christianity.[64] Not only is the conflict within the Catholic Church projected into the New Testament scene, but also Küng's own identity is reflected in his projection of Jesus. Küng is neither a bishop nor a Liberation theologian, neither a monk nor a canon lawyer. He emphatically professes being a prophetic theologian applying critically the Word of God to organized Christianity in its various forms.[65]

3. The Principles of the Kingdom

In evaluating his Church Küng establishes four principles emerging from the quadrilateral situation in the New Testament as well as in Church history. These principles emerged as the syntheses or the "sublations" of the institutional Church and its counter forces. The first principle resulted from the reaction of Christian Humanism during the periods of the Renaissance and the Reformation. The movement of Humanism did, indeed, lead to the secularist era of the Enlightenment. Yet this reaction to the Church had a beneficial effect on Western culture, as Küng observes: "It was not the Christian Churches—not even those of the Reformation—but the 'enlightenment' . . . which finally brought about the recognition of human rights: freedom of conscience and freedom of religion, the abolition of torture, the ending of persecution of witches, and other humane achievements." [66] Ultimately, though, Humanism by its ideologies of revolution or evolution led to a dehumanization of society of the most tragic dimensions.[67] Therefore, it is up to the churches to continue the humanizing process begun during the Renaissance.

Küng is firmly convinced that "Christianity and humanism are not opposites [68] as long as these forces merge in the name of Christ." [69] On other occasions he even calls the humanization of man "the precondition of true service of God." [70] In distinction from the earlier secular movements Küng calls for a "radical humanism," a humanitarian concern which was exemplified by leaders like Martin Luther King, by Pope John XXIII and by John F. Kennedy.[71] In describing this concept Küng states; "*Humanity* replaces formalism, ritualism, liturgism, sacramentalism. Service of man, it is true, does not replace service of God. But service of God never excuses from service of man." [72] The tension between institutionalism and humanism is clearly present, but it has been resolved in the principle of radical humanism.

The historical Jesus demonstrated such humanitarian concerns in the name of his Father in Heaven.[73] By his ministry he "relativized the temple and this meant the whole order of cult, the liturgy, worship of God in the strict sense of the term." [74] Jesus required first a reconciliation with the brother, and only in the second place the cultic offering of gifts. Küng remarks that Jesus was not an organization man; Jesus was neither involved in supporting the religious establishment nor in setting up a counter institution.[75] Küng rejects the traditional claims of the Roman Catholic Church that Jesus inaugurated his *ekklesia* in the hills of Caesarea Philippi, when Peter supposedly received the keys to the kingdom of heaven.

Küng agrees with contemporary theology which has demonstrated that the Church was established after the resurrection. When Jesus called himself the "Son of Man" he did not claim thereby any institutional position. Küng likes to call Jesus "the advocate" of man.[76] Jesus comes to the rescue of the common man, of the outcast, and of the public offender. By this attitude he "shattered the foundations, the whole theology and ideology of the hierarchy." [77] In following this Jesus the contemporary Christian should seek a humanitarian Church which has incorporated a radical humanism within its structure. Only along these lines is there hope for a renewal of the Church.[78]

The second principle emerges in relation to the revolutionary Zealots of Jesus' days. Küng finds similar political movements in Latin America under the tutelage of the Liberation theologians. Again the passive Church is confronted by its militant followers. From this tension the principle of "radical transcendence" should be enunciated rather than a growing polarization in the Church.[79] Küng rejects the one-sidedness of the Church as well as of the social or political activist, of the mere spiritual dimension over against the purely social approach to life. Even the Neo-Marxists have discovered their "one dimensionality" and are searching for a "socialism with a human face." [80]

Küng discovers the answer for the Church and the social activist in the principle of "radical transcendence" as proclaimed by Jesus. The Kingdom of God, also discussed in Küng's book on the Church,[81] is at once down to earth and equally beyond the grasp of man; it is visible as well as invisible, present as well as future.[82] This radical transcendence should be the synthesis of spirituality and social realism. The concept of "transcendence" should in this context not be defined in the traditional sense of "God above us," nor in the pietist sense of the "God in us," but in the eschatological sense of the "God before us." [83] The advent of God's Kingdom was for Christ and should be for us an imminent reality which is coming to us in spite of any human effort or revolution.

Radical transcendence requires therefore a radical conversion, a new way of thinking and acting. It is in the context of social realism that Küng comes to speak about the personal decision for Christ as a commitment to the realization of the kingdom of God:

> What does this mean for man? That *he cannot take existing things in this world and society as definitive.* That for him neither the world nor he himself can be the first and the last. That the world and he himself simply as such are utterly relative, uncertain and unstable. That he is therefore living in a critical situation, however much he

likes to close his eyes to it. He is pressed to make a final decision, to accept the offer to commit *himself to the reality of God,* which is ahead of him.[84]

This hope in God's future allows, even assigns the Christian to interpret the world and its history and accordingly to criticize and transform society. Neither the maintenance of the status quo nor a revolutionary social change can be justified in the light of God's future kingdom. A transcendent view of the world will have its own transforming impact on society; a genuine hope for God's future will determine the present. Jesus rejected the mere visionary apocalyptics as well as the militant Zealots. It is the synthesis of ecstasy and crusade which creates the nonviolent social transformation advocated by Jesus, and in our generation by men like Gandhi and Martin Luther King.[85]

Thus modern man finds two principles delineated in the sociological context of the historical Jesus: First, the principle of radical humanization in tension with the authoritarian religious establishment, and second, the principle of radical transcendence as a synthesis of utopian ecstasy and militant social activism. A third principle emerges in discussing the ascetic withdrawal practiced in Jesus' day by the Essenes and by the earlier Qumran community. Throughout the almost two thousand years of Christian history many similar movements followed the example of the Qumran. They all reacted to the worldliness of religious people and withdrew into solitary places to establish a holy community.

Again Küng discovers in the ministry of Jesus a Hegelian synthesis of two contrasting lifestyles, of worldliness and other-worldliness, of attachment and detachment. A relevant historical example was given by Küng in an earlier publication,[86] where he portrays the English humanist Thomas More. Externally deeply involved in politics and in his legal profession More proves to be inwardly free from desires to power and material wealth. Such a detached involvement with society and one's neighbor is called an attitude of "radical love" by Küng.[87] In contrast to the selective love of the Essenes Jesus loved every human being. On the other hand, instead of a general mystic love, e.g. of a Gautama Buddha, Christ practiced a concrete love for a particular neighbor. "Radical love" then is the synthesis of selective love and mystic love, of particularism and generalism, of exclusivism and inclusivism.

In the biblical context "radical love" is enunciated especially in the encounter with the separatistic ascetics. Jesus mingled with the masses as he was healing, encouraging and forgiving those who were rejected by society and by the religious elite. Jesus' ministry of humble service stood in sharp contrast to the principles of the Qumran community. Where they said: ". . . no blind man, or maimed, or lame or deaf man, and no minor, shall enter into the Community . . . ," Jesus testified: "The blind see and the lame walk, the lepers are cleansed and the deaf hear. . . ." [88] Where the Qumran required hating one's adversaries, Jesus upheld as the highest axiom a radical love for the enemy.[89] While religious ascetics of all eras were seeking external detachment of sin and worldliness, Jesus by contrast advocated an inner detachment from overt sins like sexual abuse or murder.

Many monastic leaders have claimed Jesus' command to the rich young ruler, to give all he had to the poor, as a challenge to a deeper level of religious life. Küng interprets this passage, however, as an incidental instruction. The radical love of Christ does not require a vow to an ascetic and celibate life but is: "In the first place and for the most part a question of behavior in *ordinary life:* who is first to greet the other, what place we seek at a feast, whether we are quick to condemn or judge compassionately, whether we strive for absolute truthfulness. . . ." [90]

Radical love means a life of forgiveness, service and renunciation. None of Jesus' instructions should be interpreted in a legalistic manner. Radical love is a voluntary commitment aiming at concrete acts of disinterested service; for instance, going the second mile with the person who already has forced me to go one mile or presenting the left cheek to him who has already struck me on the right cheek. Such examples indicate that Jesus did not see these admonitions as legalistic applications of the Law. Rather, they were "borderline cases" illustrating what might be needed in some situations. Radical love exceeds the selective love of the Essenes and later communal movements, because it expects each Christian in any situation to demonstrate the love of God.[91]

The adjective "radical" derived from the Latin word "root" certainly is a favored term by Küng.[92] After having delineated the principles of radical humanism, radical transcendence and radical love he lastly discusses the concept of radical obedience in contrast to the legalistic righteousness of the Pharisees.[93] As was mentioned above Küng parallels these rabbis to the ecclesiastical canon lawyers of today. He blames the latter in particular for the most unfortunate encyclical against artificial birth control issued in the year 1968.[94] Like the contemporary canon lawyer the historical Pharisee lacked a sense of proportion and realism. To the Pharisee legal consistency was more important than the well-being of mankind.

A New Testament example was the discussion concerning the Sabbath. The Pharisees criticized the disciples of Jesus when they had been plucking some ears of grain on the Sabbath day. Jesus used this occasion to state bluntly his view of obedience to the Law: "The Sabbath was made for man, not man for the Sabbath." [95] In applying this maxim to all of God's revelation Küng states: "From the first to the last page of the Bible, it is clear that God's will aims at man's well-being at all levels. . . . God wills life, joy, freedom, peace, salvation, the final, great happiness of man." [96]

In referring to the Pharisees Küng is not only reminded of Vatican policy but also of common Catholic life with its penitential practices.[97] The Scriptures, in Mark 1:15, call for a *metanoia* which means a change of mind or a different way of thinking. Yet, under the influence of the custom of penance, Catholic and also Protestant translators have rendered this passage: "repent, and believe the Gospel." [98] Küng knows from experience the psychological benefit a penetential obedience provides: "A law provides security, because we know exactly what we have to keep to: just this, no less (which can sometimes be irksome) but no more (which is sometimes very congenial). I have to do only what is commanded. And what is not forbidden is permitted. And there is so much we can do or omit in particular cases before coming into conflict with the law." [99]

But this lifestyle creates an attitude of hypocrisy or of "compromise" as Küng calls it. "It is precisely this legalistic attitude however to which Jesus gives the *deathblow.*" [100] In quite Protestant fashion Küng proceeds in affirming that Jesus challenges us to a life of radical obedience to the will of God. In this connection he avers that the common denominator of the Sermon on the Mount as well as of the Lord's Prayer is that God's will be done.[101] Thus the contemporary Christian is admonished by Küng stating that "God's will is not simply identical with the written law and still less with the tradition which interprets the law." [102] The will of God challenges the total man for the well-being of all mankind.

Thus the quadrilateral polarity of Sadducee, Zealot, Essene and Pharisee has yielded a set of principles which should guide the contemporary Christian in his personal situation. It is evident that Küng warns for traditional Christian lifestyles as they manifest themselves in ritualism, pietism and legalism. But what does Küng have to say to the totally non-Christian or nonreligious person? However much the disenchanted Christian needs encouragement and guidance, the great commission to evangelism and missions is equally strong in the Scriptures. In his book *On Being a Christian* Küng remains basically the theologian of reform and renewal. He presupposes the German or European ecclesio-political scene and has little to say to the needs of the Third World or to the unchurched masses in the great metropolitan areas of the world.

Even if the "Great Commission" of Matthew 28:19–20 is left out of consideration, did Jesus not call for a going out "to the highways and hedges" (Luke 14:23) or for a being sent "as sheep in the midst of wolves" (Matt. 10:16)? Should Küng not have communicated these missionary challenges to the Christians who are as yet not disenchanted? Evangelical Protestants may have overstressed evangelism and missions, but these ministries certainly cannot be omitted from a picture of the historical Jesus. However helpful Küng's sociological analysis of the New Testament may be, the reader cannot avoid the impression that Küng has used his own situation as the sole hermeneutical key to his interpretation of the Scriptures.[103]

4. The Realization of the Kingdom

The culmination of the Gospel story is the victory of Christ over his enemies who represent the powers of darkness.[104] This means that for Küng the "saving event" is the event of the resurrection rather than the agonizing event of the crucifixion. The cross remains essential also for Küng, because "it is the permanent signature of the living Christ"; it identifies a savior involved in "changing life and social conditions here and now *before* death." [105] But the focus of attention in the New Testament is on the resurrection, according to Küng.

Therefore, not only the event of the crucifixion but also the institution of the Last Supper are to be reinterpreted. Küng rejects the traditional celebration of the Last Supper as "the sacrifice of the

Mass," which according to Catholic dogma repeats or extends the sacrifice of the cross.[106] Instead of a sacrificial interpretation of the Last Supper he subscribes to a eucharistic interpretation, namely as a messianic meal celebrated with the living Lord. The bread and wine reaffirm the new covenant established in his blood but manifested in his resurrection. "It should therefore not be celebrated as a meal to satisfy hunger, oriented to the past, but as a meal of messianic hope pointing forward and calling to action." [107]

The cross represents the historic conflict with the representatives of human society.[108] It could not have been avoided since Jesus lived and worked in tension with all levels of society. "For the silent majority he was too noisy and for the noisy minority he was too quiet, too gentle for the strict and too strict for the gentle." [109] Küng states repeatedly that Jesus consciously provoked the leaders of his day.[110] As a result "the system" killed him with the help of the Roman officials.[111] In the end Jesus was charged with creating political unrest which definitely was a false accusation and "a cover for the religious hatred and envy of the hierarchy and their court theologians." [112] The very use of this terminology indicates that Küng also includes the cross and the resurrection in the socio-religious parallelism between the New Testament era and the contemporary situation.[113]

Thus the crucifixion was caused by the powers "from below," namely by the antagonistic parties surrounding Jesus, which is in stark contrast with the verticalist Anselmian interpretation of the cross as a substitutionary atonement to God on behalf of man's sin.[114] According to Anselm, God's honor was offended by the original disobedience of man. The atonement of this sin required the shedding of the blood of the perfect lamb, Jesus Christ. Whatever would happen later in Jerusalem, the atonement was needed ever since the Fall for God's sake—it was necessitated "from above." Because of Küng's opposing view he does not use the term *substitution* for the work of Christ but rather the concept *representation*. He means by this first of all that Jesus was a "representative of men before God." [115] The cross was erected because of the actual sins of man not because of the original sin of Adam and its consequences. "What is removed is not God's personal animosity, but that real enmity between man and God which has its origin, not in an inherited sin, but in actual, personal guilt and the universal burden of sin." [116] Küng remains

consistently and consciously a theologian *from below,* up to the point
of the resurrection.

With the account of the resurrection Küng abruptly shifts to a
theology *from above.* [117] The initiative is no more taken by human
leaders or by a historical Jesus, it is God who takes sides in the
quadrilateral conflict around Jesus. "God acknowledged him and
not the Jewish hierarchy." The resurrection demonstrated that Jesus
"was right in setting himself above certain customs, prescriptions
and precepts." "He was right too in identifying himself with the
weak, sick, poor and the underprivileged."[118] The supposedly false
prophet Jesus was declared to be the Messiah. He was revealed as
God's messenger and as the advocate of man.[119] It was only after
the resurrection, according to Küng, that the great distinctive titles
were given to Jesus. From that moment on he was clearly the *Kurios*
or Lord, "Son of David" and "Son of God." Jesus Christ became
then himself the focus of the proclamation rather than just his words
and deeds. It was the experience of the living Christ which meant
the beginning of the Church and its mission.

Father Avery Dulles stated in the scholarly journal *America:*
"Küng's account of the rise of the Easter faith is in my judgment
both persuasive and inspiring." [120] On the other hand, the Jewish
scholar, Dr. Samuel Sandmel, questioned whether Küng's interpretation "bears any real relationship to what the word resurrection would
ordinarily seem to mean." [121] Küng, indeed, takes on a unique way
of interpretation. First of all, he calls attention to the difference
between the concepts of "resuscitation" and "resurrection." Jesus
was not resuscitated like Lazarus, he "did not simply return to biologi-
cal-earthly life, in order—like those raised from the dead—to die
again." [122] Jesus did not return to the realm of time and space,
which would have happened in a case of resuscitation, but he as-
cended to the Father. Secondly, Küng describes the reality of the
resurrection in transcendental terms. Jesus was "seen" and "heard,"
but such perceptions could not have been photographed or recorded.
Neither were the "appearances" described in the New Testament
visions or hallucinations,[123] but rather like divine vocations [124] as
so many Christians have experienced during later generations.[125]
Küng's third unique trait of describing the resurrection is its parallelism to the passing away of those who die in the Lord. Küng describes
the raising of Jesus Christ in similar terms: "In death and from

death he *died into* and was *taken up* by that *incomprehensible and comprehensive ultimate reality* which we designate by the name of God." [126]

The discussion of the resurrection is another example of Küng's effort to present "a rationally justifiable faith." [127] Evangelical Protestants will appreciate Küng's emphasis on the encounter with the living Lord. They will question, however, why he so carefully avoids any physical, and thereby historical, evidences of the event of the resurrection. Why does Küng raise so many disclaimers about the appearances, about the empty tomb, and about the titles of Jesus? [128] If belief in the resurrection of Jesus ultimately rests on faith in God as the creator, as Küng avers, why should he then be so anxious to present a "reasonable" faith? With the exception of his rational justifications for a resurrection faith we can agree with his affirmation: "Since God is the Alpha, he is also the Omega. The almighty Creator who calls things from nothingness into being can also call men from death into life." [129]

The kingdom of God came into its own through the crisis of the cross and by the divine affirmation of the resurrection. The historical agony of Jesus had been justified by the Father in heaven. These events constitute a pattern for the experience of a Christian. The joy of new life can only be received after a sacrifice of radical obedience; a life of sanctification can only be expected after genuine surrender to Christ as Lord. Küng observes, there always have been Christians who either seek the cross only—or merely the glorious new life. According to Küng, the apostle Paul was the only New Testament witness who understood the dialectic unity of cross and resurrection.[130] Against the enthusiasts in Corinth Paul had to preach "the word of the cross," while he had to stress the message of grace against the Judaizers in Galatia.[131] Thus faith finds its dual focus in the crucified Jesus as well as in the risen Christ.

In this connection Küng criticizes mystic and monastic movements as well as Protestant pietism because of their gravitation to mere sacrificial renunciation at the expense of constructive involvement in society. Suffering is not an experience to be endured stoically or even to be enjoyed masochistically. As Christ and the early Christians set the example of providing relief from any form of suffering so it is the task of contemporary Christians "to collaborate vigorously in the many-sided fight against suffering, poverty, social grievances, sickness and death." [132]

Resurrection faith, then, is first of all a life of Christian action. "The truth of Christianity is not something to be 'contemplated,' 'theorized,' but to be 'done,' 'practiced.' " [133] Faith in the living Lord should coincide with concrete action, [134] in particular within the realm of the Church but also in secular society. Such action is, of course, not to be confounded with any of the programs represented in the quadrilateral sociological scheme discussed above. A genuine Christian should neither affirm the status quo nor the revolution. He should neither seek refuge in withdrawal nor in juridic accommodation. [135] Christian action should be courageous because it is to be patterned after Jesus Christ, the "stumbling block."

A contemporary model for such action is Dietrich Bonhoeffer who stated in his *Cost of Discipleship:* "Following Christ is nothing else than bondage to Jesus Christ alone, completely breaking through every program, every set of laws." [136] Or as Küng concludes from the New Testament: "For Paul imitation of Christ means obedience to the heavenly Lord which has to be proved in concrete action . . . it is and remains a challenge to take up one's own cross, to go one's own way in the midst of the risks of one's own situation and uncertain of the future." [137]

The Scriptures use the Greek term *diakonia* for Christian action. Küng explains it originally meant "waiting at the tables" but translators have rendered it as "service" or "ministry." [138] Such service originally was performed by Christian men and women, rich and poor, educated and noneducated. Küng deplores the historical development of a special class of ministers and its attendant consequences. More devastating still was the concept of "hierarchy" meaning "sacred dominion" presumably introduced by Pseudo-Dionysius by the end of the fourth century A.D. [139]

We agree with Küng that this fatal development has undermined the Christian ministry of millions of individual believers. We can understand that within this context Küng's primary suggestions for Christian action are not evangelism and mission but rather criticism, political action and participation in religious and secular pressure groups. [140] The Roman Catholic Church has reached a serious credibility gap, according to Küng. As in the days of the Pharisees so the present Vatican theologians engage in petty casuistry on sexual morals while leaving major issues, like the question of war and peace or the welfare of the masses, untouched. [141] For Küng the only hope for the Roman Catholic Church as an institution and for the spiritual welfare of its members is common action by priests and lay persons. Together they should strive "for a better liturgy, more intelligible sermons, more up-to-date pastoral care, ecumenical integration of congregations and a Christian involvement in society." [142]

What is ultimately essential for . . . *Being a Christian?* At the very end of his book Küng reaches a similar dialectic unity of effort and reward as was exemplified in Christ's cross and resurrection.[143] A life of radical imitation of the historical Jesus yields a victorious existence rooted in the living Christ. In both instances, in the life of Jesus Christ as well as in that of his followers, a Hegelian *sublation* takes place between human effort and divine recognition.[144] Through such eternal justification a Christian receives the basic trust of which Erikson spoke in his *Identity and the Life Cycle.*[145] Küng asserts that no other religion can provide this sense of confidence and personal destiny, because no other religion claims a living savior. "Only a living figure and not a principle can make sweeping demands. Only such a figure can invite, summon, challenge. The person of Jesus Christ . . . can reach a man's personal center and . . . activate that basic trust, that trust in God, in virtue of which man is capable of giving his heart to this person with his invitation and demands." [146]

A surrender to Jesus as Lord liberates man from the pressures of religious and secular society and makes man truly free. "Why should one be a Christian? . . . In order to be truly human." [147] Thus Küng returns to the initial theme of his book where he stressed the need for a humanitarian society. Christ became man in order that we might reach that same destiny through him. In contrast to the early Church which aimed for the divinization of man Küng has presented a theology of the humanization of man. Instead of proclaiming God's kingdom in Heaven, Küng proposes the need for God's kingdom on earth. "We cannot indulge in blissful dreaming of life after death instead of changing life and social conditions here and now *before* death." [148]

VII
Does God Exist?

1. Faith and Reason

Why is the Roman Catholic Church not alert to the signs of the times? Why has a "Catholic education deficit" developed? [1] Why do Catholic students "in strikingly large numbers avoid scientific-technical studies and prefer the humanities" instead? [2] Küng is of the opinion it is all a matter of long term reactionism. Frequently he refers to the ecclesiastical condemnation of the scientist Galileo in 1636.[3] The discovery of the heliocentric universe seemed a threat to the teaching authority of the Church which thusfar had accepted a traditional geocentric concept of the universe. It was ony in 1822 that Galileo's works were taken from the index of forbidden books.[4] In the meantime, however, the Church had become an enemy to the natural sciences. Quoting a German author Küng asserts that "Galileo's condemnation and the consequent loss of the world of science has not unjustly been ranked with the East-West schism and the Western divisions in faith as one of the greatest disasters in Church history." [5]

To its own detriment the Catholic Church did not listen to "the prophets" of Western culture. These men were forced to live in conflict with the Church, not because they were irreligious but because the Holy Office excluded them from the fellowship of faithful believers.[6] In his second major doctrinal exposition entitled *Does God Exist?* Küng portrays the achievements of thirty-eight scholars demonstrating in each case their good intentions. The Church, however, used the authority of God's revelation to curb the development of science and to stifle the rising tide of a democracy taking initiative in each domain of life.

A new day has dawned, however. An increasing awareness of a divine reality can be noticed among a variety of secular scholars since World War II.[7] With bold confidence Küng addressed a gathering of scholars at the occasion of the quincentennial celebration of the university of Tübingen in the year 1977.[8] The main concerns and objectives of his book on the existence of God, which was to appear half a year later, were outlined at that occasion. Küng's major thesis was that the issue of God's reality had become a viable question again. Since Kant, Christian theologians have accepted the inability to provide a rational proof for the existence of God, but since recent years also the secular philosopher has realized he cannot disprove a divine reality. Küng concludes that today we are confronted anew with "the immense relevance and the explosive power of the question of God." [9]

A striking example of this radical change in the attitude of secular scientists was the "Vienna Circle," a group of positivist scholars following the principles of the engineer-philosopher, Ludwig Wittgenstein.[10] One of his devices was: "Whereof one cannot speak thereof one must be silent." [11] Consequently the Vienna Circle banned all discussion of metaphysical reality. "Only propositions of mathematics and logic . . . and of the empirical sciences, which can be tested by experience, can be meaningful," stated their manifesto of the year 1929.[12] Nine years later Austria was overrun by the armies of National Socialism. The members of the Vienna Circle were scattered and their logical-positivistic ideas as well.

Thus Küng places himself once again as a mediator between two camps. As he had once tried to reconcile Protestants and Catholics, so he now wants to confront traditional Roman Catholic theology with secular scholarship and vice-versa. Both groups are in need of a new vision of God. At present such a vision is not found in Church dogma nor in theological scholarship but rather in contemporary philosophy. As representatives of the new horizon in philosophy

Küng suggests philosopher Karl Popper and physicist Thomas B. Kuhn.[13] Especially the latter is instructive for his model of the mutual acceptance of theology and science by his publication on *The Structure of Scientific Revolutions.*

Kuhn has demonstrated on a historical basis that new paradigms of thought emerge in a revolutionary manner channeling facts and data into a new frame of reference. If we are, indeed, approaching a radical change of outlook, theology will have to undergo a major "course correction." [14] Catholic theology especially, will finally have to abandon the medieval world picture.[15] Instead, Küng recommends an attitude of "critical rationality," which is not to be confused with the traditional approach of "ideological rationalism." "Genuine rationality is not to be equated with (the) one-sidedness and one-dimensionality" of eighteenth century rationalism.[16]

The key to the new paradigm is an absolutely new and rational way of thinking about God. To meet this challenge Küng set out to write his 700-page book on the question: "Does God Exist?" The data for this study were gathered from the history of philosophy including scholars like Réné Descartes, Wilhelm Hegel, Karl Marx, Sigmund Freud and thirty-four others. In addition to the major scholars Küng makes references to almost 1600 authors each contributing positively or negatively to the new vision of God.[17]

2. *Philosophical Analysis*

The philosophical revolution to be implemented by Christian theologians had already been prepared by the independent cavalier and freelance writer, Réné Descartes (1596–1650).[18] As an officer in the French army he observed people and situations in various countries of Europe. He took time for reflection on the philosophical questions of his day. Crucial for him, and the Western world as well, became his "Copernican experience" while watching the flames in the stove of his winter quarters in 1619. He mused that one could question the reality of every object and every power, but that the fact of one's doubting itself was beyond dispute. So the familiar aphorism originated: "I think, therefore I am." Man himself is the source of his doubt as well of his conviction.

Like the cosmological discovery by Copernicus the center of knowledge shifted 180 degrees, namely from a geocentric universe to a heliocentric. Likewise reason was not to proceed anymore from divine revelation but rather from the human mind; instead of proceeding from theocentric ideas Descartes focused on anthropocentric reason. Since that momentous night the individual is thrown back upon his own consciousness and insight. Through the experience of Descartes critical thought in the form of individual judgment has entered Western philosophy. Küng is of the opinion that Descartes provided *"a radical new substantiation of philosophy and human knowledge."* [19]

The classic book by Descartes was his *Discourse on the Method of Science,* published eighteen years after that crucial experience mentioned above.[20] Proceeding from his new position Descartes presented as his objective that the human mind should produce "clear and distinct ideas." His paradigm for this intellectual analysis was the mathematical approach which also works with clearly distinguishable entities. Applying it to human existence, Descartes isolated as his first clear and distinct idea the quality of the human mind or soul. As a second idea he considered man's participation in material reality which he called the realm of extension. Since God is pure thought and endless extension, even the existence of God could be deduced from the self-awareness of man. Thus the Cartesian philosophy hinged upon three principles: the self, matter, and God. Hans Küng has appreciation for the clarity of thought, the strict separation of revelation and reason, and the sharp distinction between philosophical argument and biblical interpretation. By his axiom and method Descartes heralded the scientific era of specialization and analysis.[21]

In spite of his importance for Western culture Descartes has been condemned by Catholics and Protestants alike as a rational humanist. In his study on the existence of God Küng wants to redress the injustice done to this pioneer of Western thought. Following his French professor, Henri Gouhier,[22] Küng lists a number of evidences of religious dedication in the reputedly rationalist scholar.[23] He furthermore shows evident parallels in the thought patterns of the normative Catholic theologian, Thomas Aquinas, and the supposedly heretical Descartes. Both men believe in the duality of nature and grace.[24] Both assume a separation between faith and reason; both consider faith an act of the will and reason an agency of the mind. Küng is well aware of the difference in objective in these two medieval men. Aquinas wanted to use reason in defense of the tradition of faith while Descartes applied it as a tool of criticism of traditional thought. It was the latter's opinion that reason should question all authority and tradition in order ultimately to reach the clear and distinct ideas necessary to gain insight in the complex reality.

It is evident on whose side Küng's sympathies are. On more than one occasion he has denounced Thomism for its noncritical acceptance of Greek ideas and its defense of the pre-Copernican view of the world.[25] Küng rejects with equal emphasis the speculations of Neo-Thomism which have developed strongly since Vatican I. Among its protagonists was one of Küng's teachers in Rome who even integrated Cartesian rationalism into his approach.[26] In rejecting an inappropriate use of Cartesian thought Küng calls for an adoption of the critical approach based upon individual judgment. This individualism is in agreement with Küng's earlier stance of a prophetic approach in the Church.[27] Quite naturally he praises the French solitary intellectual as "the initiator of the modern theory of knowledge" and as the "father of modern thought."[28]

As Protestants we can understand Küng's concern for a critical stance toward his tradition. It is not clear, however, why *individual* rational judgment should be the basis for criticism. Luther, Calvin and all the Reformers felt free to decry Rome's abuses and Aristotelian philosophy. Yet, they did not appeal to a rational subjective polemic but rather to the objective norm of the Scriptures which they interpreted within the context of their respective denominations. Even though they rejected the rationalism of Descartes, Lutheranism and especially Calvinism remained open to the new developments in science and economy.[29] The relation between religion and secular culture is more complex than Küng intimates and its improvement may need more than mere individual judgment.

Hans Küng proceeds with an elucidating portrayal of the French scientist, Blaise Pascal (1623–1662). Again he is fascinated by the individualist approach of this genius.[30] Pascal, however, aimed for a deeper level of certitude than Descartes. While the latter searched for intellectual clarity, Pascal was reaching out for the existential security of faith. Deeper than the level of mathematics is the realm of the heart. One of Pascal's best known aphorisms preserved in his *Pensées* states: "The heart has its reasons of which reason knows nothing: we know this in countless ways."[31] The strength of Pascal is his insistence on a collaboration of heart and mind, as Küng remarks: "sound reasoning (*raisonnement*) must be combined with sensitive feeling (*sentiment*)."[32]

Like Descartes, Pascal had a life-changing experience, but again

the difference is apparent. Descartes was watching the flames in a
stove where Pascal saw in ecstasy divine fire as once Moses did in
the desert. Pascal's words expressed at that occasion did not refer
to rational clarity but rather to existential certainty when he exclaimed: "Fire, Fire, God of Abraham, God of Isaac, God of Jacob,
not of philosophers and scholars . . . God of Jesus Christ . . .
He can only be found by the ways taught in the Gospel. . . ." [33]
Where Descartes gave priority to reason Pascal committed himself
first of all to the God of the Old and New Testament.[34]

Through the controversial biography on Augustine written by the
Flemish theologian, Cornelius Jansen, Pascal was deeply influenced
by Augustinian spirituality. In taking sides with the Jansenists Pascal
wrote anonymous letters against their opponents, the Jesuits. The
Augustinian concepts of the sinfulness of man and the grace of God
became also for Pascal the two polarities of human existence. Küng
observes that Pascal, because of his Augustinianism, was accepted
more widely among Protestants than among Catholics. Great followers
of Pascal were the Danish philosopher and author, Søren Kierkegaard, and the Swiss theologian, Karl Barth.

Even though Pascal was a professed Roman Catholic his books
were placed on the index of forbidden books even during his lifetime.
Hans Küng calls such a reactionary attitude of the Holy Office in
Rome a "bulwark strategy" of defensiveness.[35] On the other hand,
Küng praises the Protestant Reformation and its descendants for
demonstrating "an unparalleled new awareness of the original meaning of Christianity . . . which we in the Catholic Church began to
consider seriously only after Vatican II." [36] It is Küng's opinion
that this new awareness of personal freedom and salvation maintained
a constructive dialogue with the modern age.

After Küng's laudatory comments about Pascal and the Protestants
one would expect him to join their ranks. But he assumes instead
a critical distance from Pascal and historic Augustinianism. The disciplinary and ascetic methods of Pascal's spirituality cause Küng to
question: "Must we hate our own selves in order to love God with
all our heart?" [37] He discovers traces of similar ascetic tendencies
among Protestant Puritans and Pietists with "their depreciation of
the body and sexuality, worldly joys, pleasure, theater." [38] These
austerities are to Küng a spirituality at the expense of man. His
argument against the older Pascal and against Augustinianism in

general harks back to his rejection of the Essenes discussed in the preceding chapter.[39] Besides, the dilemma of the churches is for Küng not being solved by a change of denomination since it is for him "impossible simply to replace Thomas by Augustine, Spanish baroque scholasticism by Luther or Calvin, Vatican I by Kierkegaard or Barth." [40]

The "prophets" of the seventeenth century were still to be complemented by later scholars. The purely rational approach of Descartes would lead to a variety of rationalist movements among which Deism would play a prominent role. The strict Augustinian spirituality of Pascal would lead to a neglect of reason and a disregard of social concern through the movement of Existentialism. Needed was a philosopher who would integrate reason and personal faith and who would stimulate secular as well as religious concerns. Küng proposes for this role in modern thought the German philosopher and theologian Georg Friedrich Wilhelm Hegel (1781–1831).[41]

The ideas of this Berlin professor have challenged Küng throughout his years of study and teaching.[42] He discovered in Hegel's ideas a realistic form of Christianity open to a rational as well to a spiritual approach. Hegel "felt liberated for a new world religiosity, world piety and even world passion." [43] The doctrines of the incarnation and resurrection became two pillars in Hegel's system; through the incarnation "God is in the world" and through the resurrection "the world is in God." [44] There is a unity of spiritual and secular concern which causes an irrational faith as well as an irreligious reason to be obsolete. The absolute God brings all aspects of creation to their completion by encompassing everything and every person.

It is within the context of Hegelian thought that Hans Küng comes to the point of his book, namely to the question: "Does God Exist?" The concept of existence refers to a historical progression in time, in contrast to the static Greek concept of an unchanging God. For Hegel the ontological Greek concept of God is dead.[45] "History, it might be said, is *the* great theme of Hegelian philosophy as a whole. . . . history as realization, as dialectical process, as self-presentation and self-revelation of the Absolute." [46] Küng notes with satisfaction that God is no more merely a God of the past as the Deists professed, nor a God only of the inner man as the Pietists maintained, but He is an all-embracing God of past, present and future.

The vision of Hegel stimulated many scholars during the nineteenth

century and was appropriated during this century by the mathemati-
cian Alfred North Whitehead and the Catholic archeologist Pierre
Teilhard de Chardin.[47] From the latter are the words quoted by
Küng: "By upbringing and intellectual training, I belong to the 'children of heaven'; but by temperament, and by my professional studies,
I am a 'child of the earth.' " [48] It is this kind of world-openness
which Küng envisions as the essential aspect of the Christian faith
of the future. He finds this worldly faith lacking in traditional Catholicism as well as in Protestantism. As a lone prophet Küng challenges
his readers to a form of Neo-Catholicism,[49] which would be worldly
in its concerns but heavenly in its motivations.

Küng's philosophy can be typified by the three prophets of Western
culture: Descartes, Pascal and Hegel. The future era of Christianity
will need the rational clarity of Descartes, the spiritual devotion of
Pascal, and the dialectic unity of man's total existence related to
an absolute God as presented by Hegel.[50] This analytical, philosophical scheme should be in agreement with Küng's descriptive biblical
picture presented in the preceding chapter. The four socio-religious
options of Sadducees, Zealots, Essenes and Pharisees represent non-
dialectic sections of society. Because of their one-sidedness they can
only become part of the total divine and historical process through
the "sublation" found in Christ.[51]

3. Reaction and Challenge

"Hegel's philosophy of world history can be regarded as the foundation for the subsequent *historical presentations of art, religion and
philosophy.*" [52] Küng has to concede, however, that the same magnifi-
cent Hegel became the father of the "Left Hegelians," among whom
the leading men were: David F. Strauss, Ludwich Feuerbach, and
Karl Marx. From these leftist scholars resulted the concept of atheism
which sparked an ideology now encircling the globe. Not only was
this concept of atheism incorporated in the totalitarian movements
of Communism and National Socialism, it also had a strong impact
upon the modern sciences and technology, and even upon the developing countries of the Third World. "Anyone, therefore, who wants
to justify belief in God before the world and his own reason must
do so in face of this widespread atheism." [53]

How could Hegel's system give rise to such a vast nonreligious movement? Küng explains how Hegel's dialectic unity of God and man, of infinite and finite reality, could be reversed in order of priority. This is exactly what Ludwich Feuerbach did in his infamous publication on *The Essence of Christianity* (1841).[54] Each Christian doctrine is being turned into its opposite; instead of an incarnation process by which God becomes man, it becomes a deification process by which man becomes God. The method of this reversal issues from Feuerbach's compelling principle of projection which was widely applied not only to religion but also to such disciplines as psychology and economy. According to this theory man projects his unfulfilled desires and ideals upon an assumed divine reality. Thus Feuerbach asserted that there was no God creating man, but there was man creating God into his own image. For Feuerbach the concept of God is therefore not just fictitious but even a harmful idea, because it leads man to self-deception. Boldly he proclaimed the ultimate decline of traditional Christianity: "Faith has been replaced by unbelief, the Bible by reason, religion and Church by politics, heaven by earth, prayer by work." [55]

In refuting the principle of projection Küng follows the argumentation of the German philosopher, E. von Hartmann.[56] Its line of reasoning is that the *psychological* tendency of projection cannot be used as a *philosophical* argument against the existence of God. One might with equal justice use the universal desire for love and justice *for* the existence of God. But Küng is not satisfied simply to refute the principle of projection. The compelling force of atheism has its roots in historical circumstances. Ever since the industrial revolution religion has often extolled God at the expense of man. Küng asks rhetorically: "Is there not a broad dualistic (Neoplatonic) tradition that devalues nature, the present world and the body, running through the whole history of Christianity? . . . A spirituality hostile to the senses, expressed in a strict renunciation and humiliation of man before God that is not supported by Jesus' own teaching . . . ?" [57] No wonder that the masses reacted negatively to the ministry of the Church. Küng proposes a God who wants the fulfillment of man to his fullest potentialities. He considers atheism therefore a major challenge for contemporary Christianity to make up for its deficiencies of the past. It is for this reason that Küng has reservations against monasticism as a beneficial form of ministry to contemporary man.[58]

Another prominent Left-Hegelian was the economist, Karl Marx, who played an even more influential role than his predecessor Feuerbach. Küng endeavors creating an understanding for this German Jew who received a Lutheran education and who ended up being an advocate of atheistic Communism.[59] Through the experiences of racial discrimination and the spreading industrial revolution Marx became aware of the contextual place of man. "It is to Marx's indisputable credit to have brought out how much economic changes affect the world; . . . how great, as a whole, is the influence of economics on the history of ideas and also on the history of religion." [60]

In most disciplines man is seen today as a social being; only the Church is slow in recognizing this development. For the sake of comparison Küng provides the following data: Marx's *Communist Manifesto* was published in the year 1848, but the first Papal encyclical on social issues was promulgated only in 1891, while the Protestants with some exceptions were still later in their social concern.[61] In view of these facts Küng poses emphatically that Christianity owes a debt to industrial society. The Christian message has forever to be aware of the socio-economic implications of the Gospel and can never return to the time before Marx.[62]

One of the reasons the Marxists were not taken seriously by the churches was their adherence to the theory of atheism. Küng takes pain separating the two issues of atheism and social concern. On the basis of history he attempts to demonstrate that the theory of atheism is not an integral part of Marxist socialism.[63] Marx, Friedrich Engels, and most of their followers were, indeed, atheistic Communists. There was a time, though, when Marx himself was atheist but not socialist as there are today Marxists who are not atheist.[64] Since Marx was neither a theologian nor a philosopher his ideas concerning atheism were simply adopted from Feuerbach.

In conclusion Küng states: *"a Christian can be a socialist* (against the 'right'), *but a Christian is not bound to be a socialist* (against the 'left')" [65] As long as a Christian has a strong social commitment he has various political options. Küng positions himself "left-center" in the political spectrum by which he means "between the conservatives on the right and the revolutionaries on the left." [66] Küng says he has a genuine admiration for the Capitalist economy which has introduced great social reform programs. At the same time he is critical of the Communist party which has achieved neither freedom nor equality for its constituency and which has pacified the common man with promises more than the Church ever did. Although Marx predicted the "fading out of religion" after the great revolution it did not materialize in Russia. Christianity is more than ever a vital force in the Soviet Union.[67]

If the Church has been slow in developing a program of social concern, it has remained aloof from the area of psychoanalysis. Its initiator, Sigmund Freud (1856–1939), has received wide acclaim from admirers outside the churches.[68] This follower of Hegel shares common traits with Karl Marx. Both were Jews, both became atheists, both applied the principle of projection to their own field of study. Freud used this principle in interpreting the neurotic imagery of his patients. All of religion was considered by Freud simply as a projection of subconscious sexual drives in man. It was Freud's anticipation that successful psychoanalytic therapy would prove religion an illusion and that it would liberate man from guilt and fear better than religion had ever done.

Freud's methods of analysis included hypnosis and dream analysis. Initially his classic study on *The Interpretation of Dreams* (1900) [69] found hardly any response. It sold only 351 copies during its first six years. Like Marx, Freud suffered rejection and misrepresentation before he became famous. Küng shares this information to demonstrate the fate these men shared with prophets in any generation. In later years also Freud was proven to be right in many respects. Küng conveys that psychoanalysis was applied to literature, art, mythology, history and religion. Before long the principles and ideas of psychoanalysis became an avenue of universal enlightenment to the degree that for many people it became a substitute for religion.

Küng's reaction to Freud is similar to his response to Marx. Again he argues for a distinction between atheism and the discipline to which it is applied. He also claims that atheism is not inherently related to Freud's theory. On the contrary, Freud never became free of religious ideas and he did not win his followers to an atheistic conviction. Carl Gustav Jung even stressed the benefit of genuine religion for a harmonious personality; [70] Erich Fromm studied the variety of religious responses to gain insight into the subconscious; Victor E. Frankl believed that the psyche was motivated by spiritual forces rather than by sexual drives.[72] There is therefore no need to keep at a distance from the achievements of psychiatry. In agreement Küng quotes the French philosopher, Paul Ricoeur: "Freud has already reinforced the belief of unbelievers; he has scarcely begun to purify the faith of believers." [72]

Consequently Küng challenges especially "Protestant biblicism" and "Catholic traditionalism" to a radical course correction. There should be a "critical-dialogic cooperation" with the various medical and paramedical professions rather than a mere "peaceful coexistence." [73] With a variant on Luke 10:40 Küng remarks: "The theologian . . . can 'worry about so many things' and forget the 'one thing necessary.' " [74] If there is strong evidence of an awareness of God in the recesses of the human psyche, the Church and the theologian should relate to this in their ministry. As Christian social concern should be willing to accept directives from socio-economic theories, so Christian pastoral concern should want to benefit from the insights of psychoanalysis. Thus Küng wants to establish and extend the creative dialogue between religion and the natural sciences in all areas of life.

"God is dead. God remains dead. And we have killed him." [75] These shocking words by the nihilist philosopher, Friedrich Nietzsche (1844–1900),[76] add another dimension to Küng's review of leftist reactions to Hegel. Nietzsche reached the point of total rejection of any sensible structure of existence in following the pessimistic philosophy of Arthur Schopenhauer. The latter had come to the conclusion that "despite all Hegel's cunning, optimistic philosophy of history, this world process is without reason, without meaning or goal." [77] Did Schopenhauer still profess a form of Buddhist faith, Nietzsche's philosophy of nihilism rejected any religion and any faith in a divine involvement in the course of nature and history.

By the end of the nineteenth century all sense of harmony and meaning so masterfully crafted by Hegel at the beginning of that great century had been radically thrown aside. For Nietzsche only two concepts remained: "the will to power" and "the eternal recurrence of the same." [78] There is no progression, no history, and of course no history of salvation. In his book appropriately entitled *The Antichrist* Nietzsche asserted: "The word 'Christianity' is already a misunderstanding—in reality there has been only one Christian, and he died on the Cross. . . . It is false to the point of absurdity to see in a 'belief,' perchance the belief in redemption through Christ, the distinguishing characteristic of the Christian: only Christian *prac-*

tice . . . is Christian." [79] Nietzsche despised hypocritical, mediocre, and frustrated human beings and searched for the man of power, the later popular "superman."

This exotic philosopher is considered by Küng to be one of the "prophets" of Western culture also. What Nietzsche developed in his writings has become commonly accepted among contemporary man. Küng sympathizes with the parents who no longer know which norms they should maintain in view of their children; he understands young people who cannot find meaningful existence in a world of terror, riots, and drugs. Because of this "meaning deficit" or "meaning vacuum" [80] we are faced with a challenge to which Nietzsche alerted us almost a century ago. Küng is of the opinion that the assumption of nihilism is philosophically irrefutable, which means *"there is no rationally conclusive argument against the possibility of nihilism."* [81]

Küng is quick to add, however, that the nihilist offers no rationally conclusive argument *for* his position either. Ultimately existence is a commitment of "saying yes" or of "saying no" to reality.[82] Man can assume a positive or a negative attitude toward uncertain reality which then determines his life now and, according to our Christian faith, forever. This alternative sets the stage for Küng's great invitation covering the final and third part of his book. He challenges the reader to accept the living God, the God of Jesus Christ. Accepting this God means a total and trustful surrender involving rational, sociological, and psychological dimensions. Modern Christianity cannot return to a time before the Western prophets Marx, Freud, and Nietzsche. The nineteenth century has left a challenge to Christianity which still awaits being met during the twentieth century.

4. Affirmation and Invitation

After having confronted the Christians with the challenge raised by the Left Hegelians and by nihilism, Küng turns around, addressing himself to all those who have rejected faith in the existence of God. Since the disenchanting experiences following Vatican II Küng developed a keen interest in German Neo-Marxist philosophers. The most prominent among these were: Ernst Bloch, Jürgen Habermas, Theodor W. Adorno, and especially Max Horkheimer (1895–1973).[83] With gratification Küng observed among these scholars a growing aware-

ness of the personal needs of man which had been overlooked by
Marx in his system of dialectic materialism.

Horkheimer stated in an interview shortly before his death that
religion makes man aware: "that he is a finite being, that he must
suffer and die; but that over and above that suffering and death
there is the longing that this earthly existence may not be absolute,
not the ultimate reality." [84] Horkheimer affirmed that every person
has "a longing for perfect justice," which cannot be fulfilled within
the confines of human society and therefore transcends our history.
Man longs for "the totally other," a term which Karl Barth used
as a definition for God. Yet Horkheimer remained an atheist or at
least a nontheist as he concluded: "We cannot describe what the
Absolute is and in what it consists." [85]

Hans Küng cleverly uses the groping of his nontheistic contempo-
raries to invite secular man to a courageous reconsideration of the
potential reality of a living God. In addition to the Neo-Marxists
Küng directs his query to the rationalists among whom he considers
Dr. Karl R. Popper a viable representative.[86] This Austrian scholar,
who later was professor at the London School of Economics, became
known by his standard work on *The Logic of Scientific Discovery*
published in 1934.[87] Popper identified himself as "a critical rationalist" intimating a critical stance over against the logical positivism
of the Vienna circle and its patron, Ludwig Wittgenstein.[88]

Popper exposed Wittgenstein's principle of verification as untenable and suggested, instead, the principle of falsification. This meant
that at least a relative truth can be claimed for any fact or idea
which as yet has not been proven false or untrue. Reversely, Popper
argued that even objective scientific disciplines such as mathematics
or the natural sciences remain fallible as long as not all data have
been verified. Since each project of scientific research or religious
investigation has to proceed from a hypothesis or a conjecture, "an
irrational choice" [89] has to be made.

Küng, of course, welcomes this line of reasoning since it restores
the place of theology within the academic community. As a theologian
one has to proceed from the premise that reality is created and
upheld by the living God. Even though this premise is far from
arbitrary, it is nonetheless not a logic proof but an act of faith
from which one proceeds.[90] In this connection Küng quotes Hegel
who long before Karl Popper had declared that the first condition

of philosophical study is "faith in reason, trust and faith in oneself
. . . faith in the power of the Spirit." [91]

Thus the Neo-Marxist has discovered a longing for "the totally
other" and the rationalist has recognized the need for an initial
premise in any area of human research. Even a contemporary positivist like Wolfgang Stegmüller has to concede: *"we must believe something from the outset to be able to talk of knowledge or science at
all."* [92] Thus the theologian has received space to work on his concept
of the existence of God and to present the premise of a personal
faith to his reader or audience. Küng uses the words of Dag Hammar-
skjöld, the first secretary general of the League of the United Nations,
as the guiding thought in his discussion of the premise of basic
trust: *"I don't know Who—or what—put the question, I don't know
when it was put. I don't even remember answering. But at some moment
I did answer Yes to Someone—or Something—and from that hour I
was certain that existence is meaningful and that, therefore, my life,
in selfsurrender, had a goal."* [93]

Thus Küng invites his readers "to say yes" to reality, yes to
God, yes to the God of Jesus Christ. Psychoanalysis has demonstrated
how beneficial an attitude of trustful surrender can be and equally
how detrimental the mood of distrust can be for man's physical
and emotional well-being. Küng briefly reviews the studies of Erik
H. Erikson and other psychoanalysts [94] who have experimented with
infants and children. They demonstrated that even the stage before
birth has a decisive influence on the development of a fundamental
trust in the child and later in the adult.

By presenting this information Küng wants to win his readers
for a conscious and rationally justifiable decision to a fundamental
trust in the God of life. Again, this rationality is not based on a
strict, logical argument but on the pragmatic consideration of what
man could either win or lose by a commitment to a fundamental
trust or distrust. At this point Küng's position is similar to Pascal's
wager argument.[95] The latter reasoned one could never lose in wager-
ing on the existence of God. If, per chance, God might not exist
one would not have lost anything at the moment of death. What
Pascal held out as a gain or loss for eternity, Küng presents as a
benefit or detriment for this life in the first place.

Therefore, man has to face up to the great alternative. At this
point Küng quotes Shakespeare's aphorism: "to be or not to be,

that is the question." [96] He also likes to refer in this connection to the great Danish author and theologian, Søren Kierkegaard,[97] who enunciated "the risk of freedom" or "the leap of faith." Since World War I an increasing number of theologians and philosophers have developed this concept of an existentialist decision. Küng joins the position of these scholars by reminding his readers repeatedly that they are free to choose. God grants man the basic freedom of choice which somehow is interwoven in his decree of prevenient grace. For all practical purposes, though, man is free in determining his own commitment. As Küng states: "Within the limits of innate dispositions and environmental determinants, man is free: free as opposed to dependent on power and force, free in the sense of self-determination, of autonomy." [98]

This freedom of choice is again backed up by a pragmatic argument. "In the last resort, it is not an external proof of freedom, but my own, inward *experience of freedom*, that tells me that I am free." [99] Küng is not interested in arguing with Augustine or Calvin about original predestination—and he does not want such theological issues to interfere with the contextual situation of man. For Küng freedom is an experience gained in the actual process of decision-making; he compares it to the experience of learning to swim. The instruction is helpful but the actual confidence and skill is gained by simply jumping into the water.[100]

Küng is careful not to identify fundamental trust with the biblical faith in the revelation of the God of Jesus Christ.[101] Philosophy may speak about the absolute ground of being, the Bible speaks about a God with a name.[102] Already Pascal made a clear distinction between the God of the philosophers and the God of Abraham, Isaac, and Jacob.[103] A similar issue is at stake in the comparison of biblical religion and the world's living religions. Küng dismisses an outright rejection of these religions since they express in a variety of ways a genuine concern for mankind;[104] they search for forms of righteousness, love, and security.[105] Such evidences of God's general grace are indications to Küng that adherents of non-Christian religions can gain eternal salvation. Küng adds, however, one proviso that *"the question of salvation . . . be distinguished from the question of truth."* [106] He explains that their concept of God is unclear; they either have no personal God as is the case with Confucianism and Buddhism,[107] or they have many gods as in the case of Hinduism.

Küng is of the opinion that because their doctrine of God is unclear these religions have no historical destiny.

The God of the Old Testament, who is shared by Jews and Moslems, is directly involved in nature and world history as well as in the history of salvation. Such involvement also means the working of miracles.[108] Küng explains that "involvement" may not necessarily mean an interception of natural laws even though modern science is increasingly willing to accept this. The theory of absolute causality has been replaced by the "complementary theory" which allows for a coexistence of necessity and chance, for causality and intervention at the same time.[109] Küng prefers to stress the wondrous work of God rather than miraculous manifestations: "God is not forced to present a great spectacular show of 'miracles' . . . God's greatness consists not in the fact that he can or must be able to do this, but in the fact that he has no need of it, that he can do without spectacular effects." [110] Küng asserts that God's dealing with man can occur in human life without interception of any natural law or historical circumstance.

Also the discussion of an absolute beginning and end to the existence of this globe has become a viable option again.[111] Various theories remain but the biblical stories of the creation and consummation are not totally at odds with modern science anymore. Modern exegetes of the Scriptures are reminded by Küng that the Bible is not a book of scientific analyses or prognoses. Küng points out that *"The language of the Bible is not a scientific language of facts, but a metaphorical language of images."* [112] Küng chides his colleagues, the Catholic "court theologians," for continuing to rely on the medieval proofs for the existence of God and his creation. Faith in God the creator cannot be based on rational Neo-Thomistic argument anymore.[113]

At this point Küng invokes Martin Luther as he denounced scholastic theology as the bewitching "whore reason" or as the "charlatan Aristotle." [114] On the other hand faith should remain "rationally justifiable," at which point Küng would disagree with Luther as well as with Barth in our era. Küng wants to maintain a middle position between the Neo-Thomistic natural theology of Vatican I and the dialectic theology of Barth.[115] "The right way, then, would lie between the purely authoritative assertion of God in the spirit of dialectical theology and the purely rational proof of God in the spirit of natural theology, would lie between Karl Barth and Vatican I." [116]

And this way is for Küng the Hegelian dialectic of revelation and reason, of the subjective idea verified by objective logic. Küng concludes his long quest for the existence of God with the words: "The important thing was and is to see the relationship in a truly dialectical way. In the God of the Bible, the God of philosophers is in the best, threefold sense of the Hegelian term 'sublated'—at one and the same time affirmed, negated and transcended." [117] In simple pragmatic language, Küng wants to take the Bible seriously but he wants to demonstrate at the same time how much common sense it makes to believe in God. Küng wants to give a listening ear to scholars of all disciplines in order thus to be able to provide the most rationally justifiable defense of the ultimately irrational act of faith in the living God. [118]

In sum, we may take note that Küng's quest for the existence of God is basically an apologetic affirmation of the Christian faith. He is to be applauded for the enormous range of sciences and historical detail he covers in order to present the rational feasibility of the premise of God's existence. Our brief survey should invite the reader to gather more details on any of the topics discussed in this chapter. Küng's most original and creative work has been done in the field of apologetics, especially in his encounter with contemporary scholars.

This apologetic presentation is, however, marred or confused by Küng's ongoing polemic with the Roman Catholic Church in particular and with Christianity in general. The Catholic leadership is accused of clinging to a medieval philosophy and its corresponding outlook on life. The secular prophets Descartes, Pascal, and Hegel, have a message for traditional Christianity; even the atheistic scholars, Feuerbach, Marx, Freud, and Nietzsche, hold out a challenge to contemporary Christianity. Küng wants the Church to wake up to the twentieth century, where there are psychoanalysts, natural scientists, and logical rationalists groping for an ultimate principle of existence, for a divine ground of being.

While we agree with Küng in the need for facing up to an all-inclusive challenge of ministering to contemporary man in his complex twentieth-century situation, we would assume that the new paradigm, of which Thomas S. Kuhn spoke,[119] would involve more than the fulfillment of German philosophical theology. The renewal of the Church will need sound academic leadership but also the not so pragmatic spirituality of those who withdraw from the busy marketplace of life.

VIII
Hans Küng As Theologian

Summarizing our study of Küng's work, three aspects of his personal approach emerge. In this concluding chapter we will deal first, with the fact of his disqualification as Roman Catholic professor; second, with the style and method of his theology; and third, with his position as representative of Neo-Catholicism.

1. Hans Küng—A Discharged Theologian

December 18, 1979, came as a complete surprise and shock to Hans Küng who had just arrived in an Austrian ski resort for his Christmas holidays.[1] On that particular day the papal messenger delivered at his home in Tübingen the fateful declaration of his disqualification as Catholic professor. Before the end of that year Küng had received the withdrawal of his "missio canonica" enacted by the local bishop, Msgr. Georg Moser.[2] This decree meant that Küng could forthwith not give instruction to Catholic students preparing for the priesthood or for an academic profession in service of Catholic institutions.

In a later interview Küng described his resulting frustration: "For months I was not able to do anything. Every morning I was sitting behind my desk but could not get one syllable on paper."[3] Küng considered himself a victim of spiritual inquisition since he was condemned without a hearing and without the opportunity to defend himself. He blamed his sudden dismissal upon the reactionary policy of Pope John Paul II who had disciplined or censured several scholars during the preceding year.[4]

Küng had aggravated the situation by releasing a public evaluation of the Pope's first year in office, and *The New York Times* published Küng's "interim appraisal" on October 19 of that crucial year, 1979. Somewhat insolently he had stated: "I am convinced that John Paul II, who is certainly not lacking in Christian self-confidence, will be able to take unbiased note of my *correctio fraterna.*" Although the Chancery Office of his diocese declared that this article had been of no influence,[5] the fact remains that Küng received his dismissal exactly two months later. After voluminous correspondence and intensive meetings Küng finally accepted a partial resignation on April 8 of the following year.[6] His directorship of the Institute for Ecumenical Research was to be maintained and he would be allowed to teach under the direct supervision of the Senate of the university, which meant Küng would be no more part of the Catholic faculty.[7]

Popular reaction to the concerted action of the Vatican and the German bishops against Küng was enormous. Küng himself received over 5000 letters of support while the German Bishop's Conference and the Vatican received "thousands upon thousands" letters of protest.[8] Students paraded in large numbers through the streets of Tübingen and attended his open lectures in droves. Küng's tour through the United States almost a year later drew large crowds at every occasion.[9] Küng remained firm in his intention to be a Catholic theologian working for change and renewal of his Church.[10] Incessantly he hammered away at the issues which were not taken up at Vatican II: the moral issues of birth control, celibacy, and divorce but equally the ecclesiastical issues of papal infallibility, ordination of women and Marian devotion.[11]

In his publications Küng remained the apologist for the Christian faith extricating himself increasingly from polemics with his superiors. Already in the year 1978, around his fiftieth birthday, Küng confessed: "I have honestly had enough of continually defending myself against bishops and their tame theologians. . . . What honestly fascinates me is everything that is of significance for us theologians today in astrophysics, in atomic theory, in microbiology, in psychoanalysis, in philosophy and scientific theory—but also in literature, art, and music." [12] But in his polemics as well as in his apologetics Küng did not develop new ideas since 1979, undoubtedly because of personal circumstances.

A small booklet appeared during the first year of his dismissal entitled: *Art and the Question of Meaning.* A footnote states: "the philosophical-theological substantiation of the basic conception largely taken for granted here is found in . . . *Does God Exist?*" [13] Küng demonstrates the socio-political dimension of art and challenges the artists to a role of humanitarian service in an increasingly inhumane society. Art can express a sense of basic trust or mistrust, it can depict the beautiful and harmonious as well as the ugly and meaningless aspects of life. Küng expresses the hope that art may symbolize "the still hidden, incomprehensible great mystery in us and around us: that is, the suprasensible ground of meaning of all our reality in the midst of the world of sense." [14]

Also he wrote a theological volume completing the trilogy which includes *On Being a Christian* and *Does God Exist?* It is basically an application of the previously gained principles to the recent concern on death and dying initiated by Dr. Elisabeth Kübler-Ross. [15] Küng's volume bears the title: *Eternal Life? Life After Death as a Medical, Philosophical, and Theological Problem.* [16] It represents the sensational open lectures of the summer of 1981 and is dedicated to all those who "enabled me to survive intellectually and finally to continue working at theology." [17] The focus of this publication is the resurrection of Christ and its meaning for our experience of dying. Like the resurrection of Christ so is our death a transition to a higher plane of life; the prospect of dying should therefore enhance, in the Christian, the sense of basic trust. To believe in an eternal life means for Küng "to rely on the fact that I shall one day be fully understood, freed from guilt and definitively accepted and can be myself without fear." But it also means that he therefore "can work for a better future, a better society, even a better Church, in peace, freedom and justice." [18] Quite appropriately for Küng's own situation he closes with the words of Revelation 21 and 22: "You see this city? Here God lives among men. He will make his home among them: they shall be his people, and he will be their God; his name is God-with-them. He will wipe away all tears from their eyes; there will be no more death, and no more mourning or sadness. . . . They will reign for ever and ever." [19]

2. Hans Küng—An Editorial Theologian

What makes Küng such a popular author, lecturer and professor? Robert Nowell is correct in highlighting Küng's "passion for truth." [20] In his lectures and articles Küng, indeed, did raise the question of "truthfulness" or "believability" of the Church and Christianity. In a similar vein Leonard Swidler refers to Küng's "honesty" by which the concepts and customs of his own church are questioned.[21] In a general sense, though, each scholar raises the question of truth involving mostly criticism of traditional patterns of thought. There must be other reasons for Küng's popularity.

When reading or listening to Küng one is always struck by his timeliness; he talks and writes about issues which have everyone's interest at that particular moment. Some reviewers have called him therefore an "editorialist." Küng began his publicity in writing on the concept of justification by faith when the ecumenical discussion was at its height. He then continued with historical studies on *The Council and Reunion*, thus focusing upon the approaching Vatican Council.

As was mentioned above, Küng's book on the Church was written in competition with the Vatican fathers.[22] His various articles and meditations on the priesthood, celibacy, freedom in the Church, and so on were all commenting on current questions in his Church. Another aspect of this timeliness of Küng's method is his careful planning of dates for publication. For example, his most inflammatory book on the question of infallibility was issued on 18 July 1970, the very day of the centennial of its original definition. In the same year Küng's Hegel edition was published at the occasion of the bicentennial of Hegel's birthday.[23]

Such editorial theology which is characterized by incidental expositions of current issues in the light of history and the Scriptures may be motivated by a pastoral concern for the public, but it does have its drawbacks from a systematic theological viewpoint. Küng's major work, *On Being a Christian*, was highly relevant in comparing contemporary ecclesio-social structures with the New Testament world of Jesus. But because of this focus on the socio-religious context of the historical Jesus, Küng's book was far from a "summa" on salvation and Christian life.[24] Küng was unjustly criticized for presenting a "hippy style" Jesus,[25] but the anti-establishment tenor of the sixties weighed heavily upon the pages of his presentation of being a Christian. In his second major theological study on the question: *Does God Exist?*, the discussion of God's existence is to be praised for its apologetic value but it certainly is not an exhaustive presentation of the essence and revelation of God. The third volume of his theological trilogy dealing with "eternal life" picked up on the popular discussion on death and dying, but remained aloof from all other aspects of eschatology.

Küng has rejected his identification as an editorial theologian at various occasions. In a recent interview he objected: "I am not a theologian who caters to the latest fashion having to write an article as soon as something new is asserted. Twenty years of research have preceded my book on *Does God Exist?* No, I do not belong to the modern cocktail theologians." [26]

As we have demonstrated in this book Küng certainly is correct in stating that he draws upon insights gained over a long period of study. Nonetheless at the moment of writing a book or preparing for a lecture he selects from his resources and tailors it very closely to the current need of his readers or audience. His popularity has demonstrated that our modern era needs such editorial theologians who can guide the public and the news media in the ever-changing succession of issues. Several of these theologians have created their own journal in order to communicate on a continuing basis. Reinhold Niebuhr became known in his day through his journal, *Christianity and Crisis*, while Carl F. H. Henry shaped the Neo-Evangelical movement by his bi-weekly *Christianity Today*. In more recent years Martin Marty has guided his Protestant readers on issues related to American Christianity, while Andrew Greeley provides his Catholic readers with insight into their socio-religious scene.

Editorial theology is also democratic in outlook. Theologians, like Greeley and Küng, respond to public demand rather than to a sense of normative authority or principles. Even in his theology Küng characteristically believes in the indefectability of the *people* of God while questioning the presumably infallible insight of the hierarchy. His theology "from below" directs his viewfinder to the public rather than to an eternally objective revelation "from above."

Küng's editorial theology stands out because of his inclination to speak out on all frontiers of religious thought. Küng covers in his works: New Testament studies, patristics, church history, canon law, dogmatics, philosophy, contemporary theology, science, aesthetics and ethics. There is scarcely a discipline in the humanities which Küng has not touched. It is truly amazing how many persons and facts he has marshalled through the pages of his books. The Roman Catholic Church certainly has benefited from this popular editorialist whose faithfulness to Pope John XXIII has opened up the doors of the Catholic ghetto. Yet Küng has gone too far afield losing touch with his superiors as well as with many of his Catholic colleagues. In the future he can only direct himself to the general public both in and outside of the academic community.

3. *Hans Küng—A Neo-Catholic Theologian*

In nearly each book or lecture Küng conveys his image of the ideal Catholic, or Christian for that matter. The prototype of the Christian faith and life style is to be found in Pope John XXIII and in the tenor of the first year of Vatican II when this beloved Pope was still in charge. This period reflected an openness to the past as well as to the future; a willingness to confess shortcomings and errors; and an eagerness to reach out to new structures and concepts. The key word was "renewal" and it was to be obtained by a reorientation to the Scriptures. Such an approach meant for Küng a strategy of polemics with the conservative leadership of his Church and a method of apologetics in view of disenchanted Christians. Thus Küng expects from the Neo-Catholic a willingness to speak out against the shortcomings of the Church, but also to discover a rational, justifiable faith which can enter into dialogue with the secular world.[27] The historical Jesus is a model for such a critical attitude toward traditional values and parties in the Church.

In the collection *Signposts of the Future* Küng discusses what has changed in the Catholic Church since Vatican II and how Protestants and Catholics have come closer to one another. A difference of emphasis remains: the Catholic attaches special importance to the community of faith in space and time, while the Protestant "attaches special importance . . . to constant, critical recourse to the Gospel (Scripture) and to constant, practical reform in accordance with the norm of the Gospel." [28] Küng's ideal is a combination of these two approaches which he calls "Evangelical Catholicity," and which in American context might be rendered better by Neo-Catholicity, a term also used by Küng.[29] In defining this form of faith Küng states that

"Evangelical Catholicity is finding its center in the light of the Gospel
. . . mindful of Catholic fullness." [30]

As has been shown in chapter 3 of this book, Küng also used
Congar's approach in speaking of a merger between institutionalism
and congregationalism, between a vertical and a horizontal dimension
of the Church. While Congar assigns a decisive priority to the hierarchical institution, Küng takes off from the congregational communion
in Christ.[31] His approach finds its biblical motivation in Pauline
Christianity as expressed in the Corinthian correspondence where
there are no references to bishops, elders or ordination of officers
and where every member has received his own charisma.[32]

Küng maintains there should be "no going-it-alone, either of the
'laity' without the shepherd or of the shepherd without the 'laity'." [33]
There should be no exception for women in this respect; they should
be granted access to all levels of theological education and should
have the right to be ordained to the ministry and to receive the
canonic mission to teach. Furthermore, "women should be represented in all decision-making bodies at all levels—the parish, diocesan, national and international." [34]

Within this Neo-Catholic community all members of the clergy
as well as of the laity share in the power of the apostolic succession
although each to a different degree.[35] According to Küng, a neglected
function among the participants in the apostolic legacy is the position
of the prophet or the theologian. The renewed structure of the Church
should grant a crucial role to those who have received the charisma
of distinction. The theologian supposedly has a more objective view
on issues and policies by his training in the historical critical method
of interpretation of the Scriptures as well as of the history of Christian
thought.[36]

Küng has demonstrated that the theologians had a decisive role
in the councils of the early Church and the Middle Ages up till
the fatal council of Vatican I in the year 1870.[37] It was Pope John
XXIII who restored the theologians to their rightful place within
the council by assigning them the place of "periti" or qualified advisors. But it has been Küng's experience that the theologian has
been increasingly ignored since the early days of Vatican II. This
regression of contemporary Catholicism has prompted Küng to bitter
polemics with his superiors whom he, of course, considers his colleagues in the ministry. For him, their position is backed up by

the "two-tier theory" of Thomistic Aristotelianism which supports the priority of the clergy and sacramentalist institutionalism.[38] Küng opts for the Hegelian dialectic, also used by Karl Barth, which supposedly allows new insight into the Hebraic thought patterns of the Scripture and thereby provides new direction in matters of salvation and church order.[39] Even after his dismissal as official Catholic teacher Küng still remained hopeful that he would win his Church for this Neo-Catholic position which he has maintained ever since Vatican II: "As I explained some years ago in my book on *The Church*, the expression 'Roman Catholic' is a contradiction in terms and even in these terms is of very recent origin. What is required is for Rome to be Catholic, but not for the Catholic Church to be Roman." [40]

4. Hans Küng—A Reflection

Following the life and thought of Hans Küng has afforded us insight into the pro- and regression of the Roman Catholic Church of the last thirty years. In this respect Küng is an appropriate subject since he has always been in the thick of the battle and he was usually one of the first theologians to formulate his position. Through his honest publicity he has allowed the public a look into the inner workings of the Roman Catholic Church as few before him. He has identified the issues between Rome and Reformation; between Rome and the Jews; between Rome and secularism; and, between Christianity and other religions.

Instrumental in "opening the windows" of the archaic Catholic Church following in the footsteps of Pope John XXIII, he was first among Catholic scholars to give a completely positive evaluation of the Protestant reformer, Martin Luther.[41] He is unique in his ability to reach a wide audience outside the Catholic community. And, what is most decisive for Protestants and Evangelicals, he has called his Catholic colleagues back to the priority of the Scriptures and to the Jesus of history.

Küng is a man of ideals having little patience with the managerial diplomacy of bishops and canon lawyers; he also has little understanding for conservative Protestantism or traditional Catholicism. Yet he hopes to win all Christians for a common venture of mutual understanding and courageous outreach to a world in need. Thus far his efforts, although disqualified by the Catholic hierarchy, have been welcomed by progressive Catholics and Protestants. His courageous stand against the Vatican, though, has challenged Protestants and Evangelicals of all stripes. Küng is continuing the battle of our forefathers with keen insight in the issues at stake. Küng concluded his latest public statement about the policies of Pope John Paul II with the words of Pope Gregory the Great: "But if the truth causes scandal, then it is better a scandal arise rather than the truth be abandoned." [42]

As a discharged professor of the Roman Catholic Church, as a commentator on the major theological issues of this era, and as a representative of Neo-Catholicism, Hans Küng has provided us a living and critical summary of the Roman Catholic Church. He will be remembered on the pages of history not as a Thomas Aquinas or a Karl Barth since developing a comprehensive theological system was not his forte. In our study we have discovered him as an interpreter of the issues of this century. Once this is understood, Küng's work will find its proper place among the prophets of our day. The challenge Küng presents to Catholics, Protestants and Evangelicals alike is an honest and critical approach to our separate traditions paralleled with a courageous venture to encounter our common future. He confronts us with the alternative of action or resignation, of basic trust or distrust, of faith or unbelief in the God revealed in the word and ministry of Jesus Christ.

Abbreviations

The following abbreviations have been used in reference to resource materials:

Being Christian	*On Being a Christian* by Küng
	The Council in Action. Theological Reflections on the Second Vatican Council by Hans Küng
Council, Reform and Reunion	*The Council, Reform and Reunion* by Hans Küng
Church Dogmatics	*Church Dogmatics*, by Karl Barth
The Church	*The Church* by Hans Küng
Eternal Life	*Eternal Life? Life after Death as a Medical . . . Problem* by Küng
Diskussion	*Diskussion um Hans Küng's 'Christ Sein'* by Von Balthasar
Diskussion	*Diskussion um Hans Küng 'Die Kirche'* by Hermann Häring and J. Nolte
Does God Exist?	*Does God Exist? An Answer for Today* by Hans Küng
Infallible	*Infallible? An Inquiry* by Hans Küng
Justification	*Justification: The Doctrine of Karl Barth* by Hans Küng

The Küng Dialogue

Menschwerdung

Passion for Truth

Réforme

Signposts
Structures of the Church
Truthfulness

Hans Küng

The Küng Dialogue. Facts and Documents
by the U. S. Catholic Conference
Menschwerdung Gottes. Eine Einführung in
Hegels Theol. Denken by Küng
A Passion for Truth: Hans Küng and His
Theology by Robert Nowell
Vraie et Fausse Réforme dans l'Église by
Yves Congar
Signposts for the Future by Hans Küng
Structures of the Church by Hans Küng
Truthfulness: The Future of the Church by
Hans Küng
Hans Küng: His Work and His Way by
Hermann Häring and Karl-Josef Kus-
chel

Endnotes

CHAPTER 1

1. See *Current Biography: Who's News and Why* (New York: H. W. Wilson Company, 1963), 227–28. *Contemporary Authors* (Detroit: Gale Research Co., 1975), 354–55.

2. Hermann Häring and Karl-Josef Kuschel, eds., *Hans Küng: His Work and His Way* (Garden City, N.Y.: Image Books, 1979), 29. The petition was presented by Swiss bishops in Rome.

3. Ibid., 129–30.

4. Namely: Latin, Greek, and Hebrew, and the modern languages: Dutch, English, French, Italian, and Spanish.

5. Häring and Kuschel, *Hans Küng*, 131.

6. Hans Küng, *The Church* (New York: Sheed & Ward, 1967), 24–25.

7. Quoted in Walther von Loewenich, *Modern Catholicism*, trans. Reginald H. Fuller (New York: St. Martin's Press, 1959), 207.

8. Häring and Kuschel, *Hans Küng*, 132.   9. Ibid.

10. Ibid., 135–36.   11. Ibid., 12.

12. See chap. 7 of this book.

13. Häring and Kuschel, *Hans Küng*, 135, 145.   14. Ibid., 14.

15. The final product was: Hans Küng, *Die Menschwerdung Gottes, Eine Einführung in Hegel* (Freiburg i.B., Herder Verlag, 1970). An English translation may be forthcoming. See Häring and Kuschel, *Hans Küng*, 192.

16. Küng's first article appeared in 1955; his publication on Hegel appeared in 1970. See ibid., 192, 198.

17. Ibid., 135.   18. Ibid., 133.

19. Ibid., 134–35, in theology, dialectic materialism, and sociology.

20. Hans Küng, *On Being a Christian* (Garden City, N.Y.: Doubleday & Co., Inc., 1976). See also chap. 6 of this book.

21. Häring and Kuschel, *Hans Küng*, 14.

22. Ibid., 12, 134, 151. Küng mentions Augustinus Bea, Joseph Lortz, and Yves Congar.

23. Ibid., 132, 151. It was a movement among secular priests, Dominicans, and Jesuits begun in 1943. These clergymen wanted to live and work among industrial workers in order to bring them in touch with the gospel. See Loewenich, *Modern Catholicism*, 334–37.

24. Häring and Kuschel, *Hans Küng*, 140–50.

25. Hans Küng, *Does God Exist? An Answer for Today* (Garden City, N.Y.: Doubleday & Co., Inc., 1980).

26. Häring and Kuschel, *Hans Küng*, 14.

27. *A New Catechism, Catholic Faith for Adults*, English ed. (New York: Herder and Herder, 1967).

28. Küng, *Does God Exist?*, 520.

29. Häring and Kuschel, *Hans Küng*, 151.

30. Hans Küng, *The Council, Reform and Reunion* (New York: Sheed and Ward, 1961).

31. Yves M.-J. Congar, *Vraie et Fausse Réforme dans l'Église* (Paris: Éditions du Cerf, 1950).

32. Häring and Kuschel, *Hans Küng*, 152.

33. Congar, *Vraie et Fausse Réforme*, 266.

34. Häring and Kuschel, *Hans Küng*, 151–52, where Küng explained his agreement and difference with Congar.

35. Küng, *Does God Exist?*, 518–19.

36. Loewenich, *Modern Catholicism*, 240–64.

37. The series are called: *Sources Chrétiennes*, 1942 FF, 220 vols., and *Théologie*, 1944 FF, 80 vols.

38. Also, Küng rejected the categories "nature" and "supernature" as adequate Christian categories. See Häring and Kuschel, *Hans Küng*, 140 and Küng, *Does God Exist?*, 522. This issue also became a factor of estrangement between Küng and his neoscholastic professors in Rome, see 133.

39. Küng, *Does God Exist?*, 522   40. Ibid., 521.

41. Von Balthasar suggested three themes in connection with Barth's theology. See Häring and Kuschel, *Hans Küng*, 138.

42. Küng, *Does God Exist?*, 525–27: "Tacit correction: Karl Barth again."

43. Häring and Kuschel, *Hans Küng*, 145.

44. Ibid., 39.   45. Ibid., 139.

46. Hans Küng, *Justification, The Doctrine of Karl Barth and a Catholic Reflection* (New York: Thomas Nelson & Sons, 1964), 332. For a detailed discussion of this subject, see chap. 2 of this book.

47. Küng, *Justification*, 20.   48. Ibid., 21.

49. Häring and Kuschel, *Hans Küng*, 14, 138. Von Balthasar also took care for the publication through his Johannes-Verlag and was instrumental in obtaining Barth's introductory letter.

50. The code number was 399/57i. See Häring and Kuschel, *Hans Küng*, 143–44.

51. For a listing of these materials see ibid., 187–244.

52. For a report on its holdings and research projects, see ibid., 247–54.

53. For a listing of the subjects of its forty-eight issues see ibid., 252–54.

54. Robert McAfee Brown, "On Being a Christian," *Theology Today* (July 1977):207.

55. Häring and Kuschel, *Hans Küng*, 14, 152–53. The German indication for his church in Luzern was "Hofkirche." The translation of Küng's address is: "The Church is continually to be reformed." For further details, see chap. 3 of this book.

56. Hans Küng, *Konzil und Wiedervereinigung: Erneuerung als Ruf in die Einheit* (Vienna: Herder, 1960).

57. Häring and Kuschel, *Hans Küng*, 14, 16, 152, 154. His supporters were Prelate Joseph Höfer and Cardinal König. His opponents were Professor Volk and Cardinal Döpfner.

58. Loewenich, *Modern Catholicism*, 56.

59. Häring and Kuschel, *Hans Küng*, 16.   60. Ibid., 18–19, 169.

61. Hans Küng, *Structures of the Church* (New York: Thomas Nelson & Sons, 1964).

62. Häring and Kuschel, *Hans Küng*, 158.

63. Ibid., 16, 157–60. See also chap. 4 of this book.

64. Häring and Kuschel, *Hans Küng*, 18–19, 160, 171–72. See also chap. 5 of this book. Further details are in Robert Nowell, *A Passion for Truth: Hans Küng and His Theology* (New York: Crossroad Publishing Co., 1981), 124–25.

65. Hans Küng, *Infallible? An Inquiry* (New York: Doubleday, 1971).

66. Häring and Kuschel, *Hans Küng*, 23, 172–75. See also chap. 5 of this book.

67. Häring and Kuschel, *Hans Küng*, 92.

68. Ibid., 90; in German, a "Denzinger-Theologie."

69. Karl Rahner, ed., *Zum Problem Unfehlbarkeit* (Freiburg: Herder, 1971), 376.

70. Hans Küng, *Fehlbar? Eine Bilanz* (Zürich: Benziger, 1973).

71. A collection of documents in Walter Jens, ed., *Um nichts als die Wahrheit, Deutsche Bischofskonferenz contra Hans Küng* (München: Piper & Co. Verlag, 1978).

72. Hans Küng's statements on television, 18 December and 30 December 1979. See *The Küng Dialogue*, published by the U.S. Catholic Conference, Washington, D.C., 1980, 167–68 and 181–82.

73. The tours to the United States were in Spring 1963, October 1966, Spring 1970, Fall 1971, and November 1976.

74. 1963 LL.D. by Catholic University of St. Louis; 1966 D.D. by Pacific School of Religion in Berkeley, Calif.; 1970 H.H.D. Catholic Loyola University, Chicago; and 1971 D.D. by University of Glasgow.

75. See for further details Häring and Kuschel, *Hans Küng*, 18–31.

76. Ibid., 96, 172–75.   77. Ibid., 101; see also 97–100.

78. See notes 15, 20, and 25 for bibliographical data.

79. Häring and Kuschel, *Hans Küng*, 117–23, 156, 162–67.

80. *Diskussion über Hans Küng's "Christ sein"* (Mainz: Matthias Grünewald Verlag, 1976).

81. Küng, *Does God Exist?*, 688. See also chap. 6 of this book.

82. Häring and Kuschel, *Hans Küng*, 181–82. See also chap. 7 of this book.

CHAPTER II

1. For a historical survey on the doctrine of justification, see Küng, *Justification*, 216–19.

2. For a listing of Catholic publications, see ibid., 304–5.

3. See chap. 1 of this book, sections 1 and 2; and Häring and Kuschel, *Hans Küng*, 138.

4. H. U. von Balthasar and Karl Barth, *Darstellung und Deutung seiner Theologie* (Cologne, 1951).

5. Häring and Kuschel, *Hans Küng*, 139; see also chap. 1 of this book, section 1.

6. Küng, *Justification*, 190.   7. Ibid., 202 and note 21.

8. Häring and Kuschel, *Hans Küng*, 41.

9. Küng, *Justification*, 41.

10. Häring and Kuschel, *Hans Küng*, 39.   11. Ibid., 20, 40.

12. Ibid., 43.   13. Ibid., 148.   14. Ibid., 148.

15. Küng, *Does God Exist?*, 474. See also Küng, *Justification*, 25.

16. Ibid., 44.

17. As John Macquarrie observed in the *New York Times Book Review*, 7 March 1965: "Barth does not speak for all Protestants nor Küng for all Catholics."

18. Küng, *Justification*, 195.   19. Ibid., 93.   20. Ibid., 92–96.
21. See J. Auer, *Entwicklung der Gnadenlehre in der Hochscholastik* I (1942), 109–23. Reviewed by Küng, *Justification*, 202.
22. Ibid., 202.
23. Quoted from Karl Barth, *Church Dogmatics* (IV, 1, p. 84). See Küng, *Justification*, 29–30.
24. Ibid., 197.
25. Ibid., 197, 201; cf. the title of this chapter: "Grace and Graciousness," Küng, *Justification*, 195–207.
26. Ibid., 205.
27. "The defence of indulgence became plainly a laughingstock, while I had expected it to be the main point of disputation." See *D. Martin Luthers Werke, Briefwechsel, Vol. I* (Weimar ed., 1930), 422; H. Hillerbrand, trans., *The Reformation* (Grand Rapids: Baker Book House, 1978), 73.
28. Denzinger, *The Sources of Catholic Dogma* (1955 edition), 259, canon 11. An anathema is pronounced on anyone who says that justification is based on "the sole imputation of the justice of Christ."
29. Küng, *Justification*, 6.
30. Karl Barth, *The Epistle to the Romans* (Oxford: Oxford University Press, 1932), 10.
31. Küng, *Justification*, 200. See also Küng's book on *Structures of the Church* (1964).
32. Yves Congar, *Dialogue Between Christians* (Westminster, Md.: Newman Press, 1966).
33. Küng, *Justification*, 106, 217.   34. Ibid., 106.
35. Ibid., 103.
36. Denzinger, *Sources of Catholic Dogma*, 250, no. 797.
37. Küng, *Justification*, 264; in German, the difference between "mitwerken" and "mitmachen."
38. Quoted from Migne, *Patrologia, Latin Series*, vol. 182, 1026. See Küng *Justification*, 266. See also Barth's reference to the imminent work of the Holy Spirit in man, Küng *Justification*, 234.
39. The number of seven was established by the second general Council of Lyons (1274). See Denzinger, *Sources of Catholic Dogma*, no. 465.
40. Although Luther originally left penance as a third sacrament in his *Babylonian Captivity of the Church* (1520), see *Luther's Works*, vol. 36 (Philadelphia: Muhlenberg, 1959), 18.
41. See Walter Köhler, *Dogmengeschichte* (Zürich: Max Niehans, 1951), 2:272; although he demonstrates that Luther later on became more sacramental in his interpretation (see 274).
42. See note 31.   43. Küng, *Justification*, 200.
44. Quoted in ibid., 18.

45. See Köhler, *Dogmengeschichte,* 273, referring to "numerous forms and possibilities."

46. Denzinger, *Sources of Catholic Dogma,* 244, no. 783.

47. Küng, *Justification,* 116.   48. Ibid., 118.

49. Karl Barth, *Church Dogmatics* (New York: Scribner, 1936), 1:1, par. 4, 1–3.

50. Küng, *Justification,* 111–12.

51. Ibid., 115, in accordance with B. Van Leeuwen and others.

52. Ibid., 3.

53. See chap. 1, section 2 of this book.

54. Häring and Kuschel, *Hans Küng,* 140. See also Nowell, *Passion for Truth,* 86.

55. Küng, *Justification,* 4. See also, Küng, *Does God Exist?,* 186–88.

56. Congar, *Vraie et Fausse Réforme,* 377–427. See also, 166: "Luther wanted to be the prophet proclaiming a return to the pure gospel. But because of his impassionate zeal he was unable to submit himself to a rule external to his personal experience."

57. Küng, *Council Reform and Reunion,* 74.   58. Ibid.

59. For a good exposition of the Free Church principles, see Donald F. Durnbaugh, *The Believers' Church* (New York: Macmillan Company, 1968).

60. *Martin Luther's Werke* (Weimar edition, 1928), vol. 54, 186.

61. Küng quotes St. Lyonnet, "Epistula ad Romanos" in *Verbum Domini* (1947), 117; see Küng, *Justification,* 249.

62. Denzinger, *Sources of Catholic Dogma,* 259, no. 819; reference by Küng in *Justification,* 75–76.

63. Denzinger, *Sources of Catholic Dogma,* 259, no. 822; for a discussion see Küng, *Justification,* 254–55.

64. Ibid., 40 and 41, from Barth's "Letter to the Author."

65. Küng, *Justification,* 106.

66. Barth, *Church Dogmatics,* 627; Küng, *Justification,* 79.

67. Denzinger, *Sources of Catholic Dogma,* 252, no. 800; discussed in Küng, *Justification,* 255–56.

68. Ibid., 268.

69. For Küng's study of this, see ibid., 268.

70. Quoted by Küng, ibid., 270, from "Théologie de la Grâce et Oecuménism," in *Irénikon* 28 (1955): 41.

71. From Barth, *Church Dogmatics,* IV, 2, 501; quoted by Küng, *Justification,* 70.

72. Ibid., 81, from Barth, *Church Dogmatics,* IV, 2, 584–98.

73. Küng, *Justification,* 270–71.

74. Ibid., 272; Denzinger, *Sources of Catholic Dogma,* 257, no. 810.

75. Otto Karrer, *Der Galaterbrief,* quoted in Küng, *Justification,* 273.
76. Barth chose the title *Church Dogmatics* instead of "Christian Theology." Ecclesiology has precedence over soteriology; see Küng, *Justification,* 83.
77. Ibid., 123.
78. Quoted from Barth, *Church Dogmatics,* IV, 1, 48 in Küng, *Justification,* 18–19.
79. See ibid., 125–29.
80. Ibid., 141. Rahner makes a distinction between the "appropriation" or the "possession" of the role of the second person in the Trinity.
81. Ibid., 135. See also 123, 141, 173, and 266.
82. Ibid., 139.   83. Ibid., 164.
84. See Barth, *Church Dogmatics,* II, 2, 116 and Küng, *Justification,* 14.
85. Quoted from Barth, *Church Dogmatics,* II, 2, 186 in Küng, *Justification,* 16.
86. Quoted from Barth, *Church Dogmatics,* IV, 1, 222 in Küng, *Justification,* 38. For a definition of sin, see Barth, *Church Dogmatics,* IV, 2, 389–409.
87. Christ as "the eternal mystery" in Küng's Scriptural argument based on Colossians 1:26 and Romans 16:25; see Küng, *Justification,* 127.
88. See ibid., 14.
89. Ibid., 137, see also 130–34.
90. Although see Küng's exposition of the relation of ecclesiology and soteriology, ibid., 80–91.
91. Küng uses the word of creation as an example, ibid., 213, while Barth resorts to the unity of God's act in justification and sanctification, see ibid., 70.
92. Ibid., 236.
93. Quoted from Barth, *Church Dogmatics,* IV, 1, 95 by Küng, *Justification,* 69.
94. Translation: "equally just as sinful"; Küng devotes a long chapter to this subject and asserts that Catholic theology takes the same position as long as one merely refers to contingent rather than to an ontological reality. See Küng, *Justification,* 236–48.
95. John H. Newman, *Lectures on the Doctrine of Justification* (London: Rivingtons, 1885), 57–61.
96. Quoted from ibid., 66, by Küng, *Justification,* 212.
97. Ibid., 213; see also 135–47.
98. Discussed ibid., 208–35.
99. Ibid., 221, although Küng himself speaks about the limitations of traditional Catholic doctrine on 211 and 213.

100. See ibid., 23, 6, 281, and so forth.
101. See chap. 1, section 2 of this book.
102. Küng, *Justification*, 39: "A Letter to the Author."

CHAPTER III

1. Küng has a detailed exposition on "The Ecclesiological Importance of the Council of Constance" in his *Structures of the Church*, 268–88.

2. Even Küng avoided to tackle the modernist crisis created by the "Syllabus of Modern Errors" issued by Pope Pius IX in 1864. See Nowell, *Passion for Truth*, 90.

3. During his participation in the Association of German-speaking Dogmatic and Fundamental Theologians at Innsbrück, Küng decided to enter the qualifying exam for a teaching position. See Häring and Kuschel, *Hans Küng*, 14.

4. The pope spoke in the presence of seventeen cardinals gathered in the Benedictine monastery of St. Paul on 25 January 1959, at the conclusion of the annual prayer week for Christian unity.

5. Küng is not quite clear about the origin of this phrase but assumes Calvinist derivation. See Küng, *Council, Reform and Reunion*, 9.

6. Küng was in Paris from 1955–57, while Cardinal Roncalli (John XXIII) was aspostolic nuntius in Paris from 1944 to 1953. See chap. 1, section 2 of this book.

7. See Congar's report on the "Unity Week and What It Has Meant to Me" in Yves M.-J. Congar, *Dialogue Between Christians* (Westminster, Md.: Newman Press, 1966), 17–22. The Octave of Prayer was suggested in 1907 by Fr. Paul James Francis and approved in 1916; see Paul J. Minus, Jr., *The Catholic Rediscovery of Protestantism* (New York: Paulist Press, 1976), 38–41. On Couturier, see Minus, *Catholic Protestantism*, 107–12.

8. Yves M.-J. Congar, *Divided Christendom* (London: Centenary Press, 1939). For reactions to this publication see Minus, *Catholic Protestantism*, 99–107.

9. See chap. 1, section 2 of this book.

10. Congar, *Dialogue*, 34; referring to the period 1947 to 1956. In 1954, he was denied his teaching position; see Minus, *Catholic Protestantism*, 105.

11. Congar, *Dialogue*, 31; see also Pope John XXIII. See Hans Küng, *The Council in Action* (New York: Sheed and Ward, 1963), 19.

12. Printed in Walter M. Abbott, ed., *The Documents of Vatican II* (New York: Guild Press, 1966), 3–7.

13. Also the English edition uses renewal in its text. See Cecily Hastings,

trans., *The Council, Reform and Reunion* (New York: Sheed and Ward, 1961), 208.

14. See Congar, *Vraie et Fausse Réforme* 648; see also pp. 223–28.

15. Küng, *Council, Reform and Reunion*, 51–52; see also Küng, *The Church*, 337–41.

16. See Häring and Kuschel, *Hans Küng*, 145.

17. Samuel H. Miller and G. Ernest Wright, eds., *Ecumenical Dialogue at Harvard, The Roman Catholic-Protestant Colloquium* (Cambridge, Mass.: Belknap Press, 1964), 205, 330.

18. See *Saturday Review*, 9 June 1962.

19. G. H. Duggan, *Hans Küng and Reunion* (Westminster, Md.: Newman Press, 1964), 52: "a kind of Rip Van Winkle."

20. Quoted in Küng, *Council, Reform and Reunion*, 72; expressed during the month of January 1959, in the pope's own diocese.

21. Ibid., 184. Congar requested a similar statement of repentance in his book on *Vraie et Fausse Réforme*, 588–96.

22. Hans Küng, ed., *Council Speeches of Vatican II* (Glen Rock, N.J.: Paulist Press, 1964), 146–47.

23. "For Döllinger . . . Luther was a criminal; for Grisar, a psychopath; but for Lortz, a tragic individual . . . living by faith." Küng, *Council, Reform and Reunion*, 104. Lutheranism should be called a heresy rather than schism according to Duggan, *Hans Küng and Reunion*, 19.

24. Josef Lortz, *The Reformation in Germany*, trans. Ronald Wells, 2 vols. (New York: Herder and Herder, 1968). For further information on Lortz see Minus, *Catholic Protestantism*, 115–21.

25. Josef Lortz, *The Reformation: A Problem for Today*, trans. John C. Dwyer (Westminster: Newman Press, 1968), 148. Congar had a similar evaluation in his book on *Divided Christendom*, 20: "Luther was obsessed in his longing for interior peace, for a living, warm and consoling contact with his God." Minus remarks that Franz Xaver Kiefl, dean of the Regensburg Cathedral, was the first Catholic leader to give a positive evaluation (1917), see Minus, *Catholic Protestantism*, 52.

26. Lortz, *The Reformation in Germany*, 2:342

27. Adolf Herte, *Das Katholische Lutherbild im Bann der Lutherkommentare des Cochlaeus* (Münster, 1943), 43, quoted in Minus, *Catholic Protestantism*, 205.

28. Küng, *Council, Reform and Reunion*, 74. In this connection, Küng calls Luther a revolutionary.

29. Küng, *Council, Reform and Reunion*, 74; so also Congar in *Vraie et Fausse Réforme*, 519, where Luther is paralleled with Carlstadt, Münzer, and the prophets of Zwickau who promoted their personal interpretation irrespectively of Church tradition.

30. Küng, *Council, Reform and Reunion*, 46.

31. Minus, *Catholic Protestantism*, 184.

32. Hans Küng, *That the World May Believe*, trans. Cecily Hastings (New York: Sheed and Ward, 1963).

33. Ibid., 83, 84, 133.

34. See Romans 12:1–8, 1 Corinthians 12:4–31, and Ephesians 4:4–16.

35. Gustave Weigel, "Catholic Ecclesiology in Our Time," in Daniel J. Callahan, ed., *Christianity Divided* (New York: Sheed and Ward, 1961), 177–201.

36. Dr. J. A. Möhler was church historian in Tübingen from 1820 to 1835. His first book on the unity of the Church was published in 1825, while his best known book on symbolics came out in 1832. See also Minus, *Catholic Protestantism*, 53 and Küng, *Structures of the Church*, 318.

37. Dr. Karl Adam was professor of dogmatic theology in Tübingen from 1919 to 1949. His famous work was *The Spirit of Catholicism* (1935). See also Weigel, "Catholic Ecclesiology," 179.

38. Pius XII, "Mystici Corporis," 29 June 1943 in Henry Denzinger, *Enchiridion Symbolorum*, no. 1286–91.

39. Congar, *Divided Christendom*, 75–92. The quote is from page 82. See also Congar, *Vraie et Fausse Réforme*, 103–13.

40. Küng, *Council, Reform and Reunion*, 26; quoted from J. H. Newman, *Parochial and Plain Sermons* (London: n.p., 1875), vol. 7.3., 35.

41. Küng, *Council, Reform and Reunion*, 33; quoted from Karl Rahner, *Kirche der Sünder* (Freiburg i Br:, 1948), 14. Küng does not follow Barth in his interpretation of John 1:14, which avers that Christ was identified with man's sinful nature, which would have implications for ecclesiology as well. See also Ehrlich, 234–36.

42. Küng, *Council, Reform and Reunion*, 26, 27.

43. Ibid., 34; quoted from Augustine, *Enarrationes in Psalmos*, Psalms 103; Küng interchanges individual sin and institutional corporate sin.

44. Küng, *Council, Reform and Reunion*, 12–15, 28. Congar calls the view from below the Congregationalist view. See Congar, *Vraie et Fausse Réforme*, 440–45.

45. See Küng's discussion on "Simul Justus Simul Peccator," in Küng, *Justification*, 236–48.

46. Küng, *Council, Reform and Reunion*, 28.

47. In his "German Mass," Luther expressed the desire to gather those "who want to be Christians in earnest." See Helmut T. Lehmann, *Luther's Works*, vol. 53 (Philadelphia: Fortress Press, 1965), 64.

48. See Rudolf J. Ehrlich, "Church, Scripture and Tradition" in *Rome, Opponent or Partner?* (Philadelphia: Westminster Press, 1965), 236–87. The author discusses Barth, Congar, Küng, Rahner, and Vatican II.

49. See Colm O'Grady, *The Church in Catholic Theology: Dialogue with Karl Barth* (London: Geoffrey Chapman, 1969), 279–81. For references, see "Appendix III" in Yves M.-J. Congar, *The Mystery of the Temple* (London: 1962), 288–89.

50. See Küng's discussion in *The Church*, 30–34.

51. See Küng's discussion on the "Petrine Office" in *Structures of the Church*, 224–29; and in *The Church*, 444–80, especially 451. "The Church cannot be deduced from the Petrine ministry, but the Petrine ministry from the Church."

52. Küng *Council, Reform and Reunion*, 31. Küng refers to Augustine as well as Aquinas in their discussion of Ephesians 5:27. See ibid., 29–31.

53. See Congar, *Vraie et Fausse Réforme*, 442 where he lists as the Protestant ordo salutis: Christ < salvation < church, and as the Catholic order: Christ < Church < salvation. Congar's statement again is based on Schleiermacher.

54. See the preceding sections on "Renewal Through Dialogue" and "Renewal Through Theological Reformulation."

55. Häring and Kuschel, *Hans Küng*, 158.

56. The German article was published in the *Theologische Quartalschrift* 142 (1962):385–424. Its translation appeared as a lecture to participants in Vatican II in *The Council in Action*, 159–95. See a discussion about this in Küng, *The Church*, 15–24.

57. Küng's popular book, *On Being a Christian*, uses the antiestablishment attitude of the sixties as backdrop for advocacy of Christ and a genuine Christian lifestyle.

58. For the preceding references, see *Council, Reform and Reunion*, 62–65, also 9: "Reform . . . has always *in principle* been a commonplace of Catholicism."

59. Ibid., 65–71.

60. Küng mentions only Innocent III and Leo IX in ibid., 65–67.

61. Ibid., 69.   62. Ibid., 71.

63. Ibid., 99. See also, Küng's chapter in *That the World May Believe*: "Does a Catholic have to defend everything?"

64. Congar, *Vraie et Fausse Réforme*, 220–23.

65. See chap. 2, section 2 of this book.

66. Küng, *Council, Reform and Reunion*, 86.

67. Ibid., 87, referring to the encyclical, "Inter praecipuas," 6 May 1844. See Denzinger, *Enchiridion Symbolorum*, no. 1630.

68. Küng, *Council, Reform and Reunion*, 87.

69. Ibid., 76–92.

70. See Minus, *Catholic Protestantism*, 33 and its chapter on Leo XIII, 30–36.

71. Küng, *Council, Reform and Reunion*, 92. Küng refers to Pope John

XXIII in his address to diocesan presidents of the Italian Catholic Action: "Look, brothers, this is the Church of Christ," quoted in ibid., 7.

72. Congar, *Divided Christendom*, 46.

73. Ibid., 251. The "plenitude" or the "principles" are found solely within the Catholic Church.

74. Ibid., 255. See also the instruction by the Holy Office (20 December 1949): "Things must not be presented in such a way as to give the impression that by their entry into the Church they bring her something essential which she has hitherto lacked." Quoted in Küng, *Council, Reform and Reunion*, 93.

75. Congar, *Divided Christendom*, 252.

76. Küng, *Council, Reform and Reunion*, 39.

77. Küng uses terms like "fortress" (*Council, Reform and Reunion*, 89), a "building" in ruins (ibid., 55) or a "house" fallen into disrepair (*That the World May Believe*, 39); cf. also the title of his book, *Structures of the Church*.

78. Küng, *Council, Reform and Reunion*, 100. Pope John XXIII used the concept of "homecoming" in his encyclical "Ad Petri Cathedram," 29 May 1959; see Anne Fremantle, *The Papal Encyclicals* (New York: New American Library, 1963), 323.

79. See especially Küng's section on "Christians—divided forever?" *That the World May Believe*, 77–87: see e.g., 79, "If we are not one, the world will not believe," and 81, "It's no use demanding that the others come back unless we go out to *meet* them."

80. Küng refers to worship in the vernacular, use of the Scriptures by individual believers and religious liberty in *That the World May Believe*, 83–84. Of course, his interest in Barth, Hegel, Käsemann, and many other Protestant scholars points to the same enchantment with the non-Catholic world.

81. Küng, *Council, Reform and Reunion*, 42.

82. Ibid., 86

83. Ibid., 72. For the full text of this confession, see Robert McAfee Brown, *The Ecumenical Revolution* (New York: Doubleday & Company, Inc., 1969), 98.

84. Küng, *Council, Reform and Reunion*, 97.

85. Ibid., 98. Minus quotes the French Protestant, Richard Stauffer: There is "no Protestant self-criticism corresponding to Romanist self-criticism." Minus, 205. See also Küng, *Council in Action*, 108 for mutual rapprochement.

86. Congar, *Vraie et Fausse Réforme*, 260.

87. Ibid., "Conditions d'un Réformisme Sans Schisme," 231–352.

88. Küng, *That the World May Believe*, 37; also, *Council, Reform and Reunion*, 50.

89. See chap. 1, section 2 of this book.
90. Hans Küng, *The Council in Action*, *197, 221*.
91. Küng, *Council, Reform and Reunion*, 127. See also Küng, *Justification*, 299.
92. Erasmus, *New Testament*, 1516. In his introduction, he challenged the farmer behind his plough, the weaver behind his loom, and those who walked along the road to sing about the gospel. See W. Koehler, *Dogmengeschichte* (Zürich: Max Niehans, 1951), 2:31.

CHAPTER IV

1. Hans Küng, *Fenlbar? Eine Bilanz, Eine Bilanz* (Zürich: Benziger, 1973), 321. See also Häring and Kuschel, *Hans Küng*, 172.
2. Karl Barth, *The Church and the Churches* (Grand Rapids, Mich.: William B. Eerdmans Publishing Co., 1936), 92.
3. See chap. 3, section 3 of this book.
4. Hans Küng, *Structures of the Church* (New York: Nelson & Sons, 1964). This book was an elaboration of Küng's inaugural address at the University of Tübingen in 1960. In his theological meditations, two issues were on the Church: *The Theologian and the Church* (no. 1) and *The Church and Freedom* (no. 6). Küng also gave a variety of seminars on the Church. See Häring and Kuschel, *Hans Küng*, 18.
5. See chap. 3, section 4 of this book; also Häring and Kuschel, *Hans Küng*, 157–58.
6. Küng, *The Church*, published in eight languages.
7. See Walter M. Abbott, S. J., *The Documents of Vatican II* (New York: Guild Press, 1966).
8. Häring and Kuschel, *Hans Küng*, 170–72; Küng, *Council in Action*, 84, 268.
9. Ibid. See also, Häring and Kuschel, *Hans Küng*, 169–70.
10. Ibid., *Council in Action*, 68.
11. Ibid., 73, 84, 268–69. It was not representative of the Church as a whole, had no reference to exegesis, and did not consider ecumenical viewpoints.
12. Ehrlich, "Church, Scripture and Tradition." See also Küng, *Council in Action*, 72.
13. Ibid., 262; 170–71.
14. During the second session of Vatican II, Küng underwent his first hearing on his publication of *Structures of the Church*. See chap. 1, section 3 of this book.

15. Küng, *Structures*, 74–92; "Never in the whole history of the Church was the participation of the laity so meager" as in Vatican I, 91.

16. Küng, *The Church*, 4.

17. Congar, *Vraie et Fausse Réforme*, 333–48. Congar poses the contrast between "l'adaptation-développement" to "l'adaptation-innovation."

18. Küng, *The Church*, 14. For representatives and history of Catholic Modernism, see Walther von Loewenich, *Modern Catholicism* (New York: St. Martin's Press, Inc., 1959), 54–70.

19. See chap. 3, section 3 of this book.

20. Küng, *The Church*, 43.

21. Küng has an excellent survey of interpretation over the centuries; *The Church*, 90–92.

22. Ibid., 93.   23. Ibid., 37.   24. Ibid., 34.

25. Ibid., 35.   26. Ibid., 46.   27. Ibid., 59.

28. Ibid., 96.   29. Ibid., 95.

30. Ibid., 94; although Thomas More wrote his classic *Utopia* and yet died as a martyr for his loyalty to the Church.

31. Ibid., 43.   32. Ibid., 94.   33. Ibid., 32.

34. Ibid., 81–82.   35. Ibid., 76.   36. Ibid., 80.

37. Ibid., 86. Congar goes into great detail tracing the origin, development and consequences of Protestant "Congregationalism." *Vraie et Fausse Réforme*, 440–66.

38. Küng, *The Church*, 49–54.

39. Küng, *Structures*, 77. In the early Church, the central position was occupied by the theologian, 87. The Council of Constance had 215 ecclesiastical leaders, 150 monastic leaders, and 300 theologians.

40. Küng, *Structures*, 28–39. See also the discussion on the role of the prophet in Küng, *The Church*, 432–34.

41. Ibid., 70–77, where Küng discusses the historical beginning of the Church based on studies by Anton Vögtle and Werner G. Kümmel.

42. Ibid., 119. Küng's exposition of the concept "people of God" covers the pages 114–32. Küng follows A. Oepke, H. J. Kraus, R. Schackenburg, and others.

43. Ibid., 116.

44. Ibid., 120–21; quoted from Romans 9:25 and Acts 15:14.

45. Küng, *The Church*, 107–11.

46. Ibid., 122; references to Hebrews 4:9, 11:25, and 13:12.

47. From the Greek "Klyros" meaning "share" or "lot" and "laikos" indicating the uneducated masses. Küng, *The Church*, 385.

48. Ibid., 125–28. Also rejected on this basis are the "hypostazation and idealization" of the Church. See ibid., 129–32.

49 Ibid., 138; discussion of the Jews in 133–50.

50. Quoted in ibid., 137. See further Abbott, *Documents of Vatican II*, 663–68.

51. Küng, *The Church*, 149.

52. Ibid., 187–88 and a discussion on 225–27. The concept "body of Christ" should not be considered ontologically, according to ibid., 229–37.

53. Ibid., 179.   54. Ibid., 187.

55. See also 1 Timothy 6:20 and 2 Timothy 1:6; discussion in Küng, *The Church*, 179–80.

56. See Hans Küng, " 'Early Catholicism' in the New Testament," in *Council in Action*, 176–81. In this article, Küng is decisively more institutionally oriented than in his later book on the Church.

57. Küng, *The Church*, 180.

58. For definition and relation of services, charismas and vocation, see ibid., 188.

59. Ibid., 226.

60. On baptism, eight pages, and on the Lord's Supper, fourteen pages; ibid., 203–24.

61. Ibid., 207.

62. Ibid., 23–24. Louis Bouyer and Congar accuse Küng of a kind of Biblicism or "Corinthism." H. Häring and J. Nolte, *Diskussion um Hans Küng "Die Kirche"* (Freiburg: Herder, 1971), 46, 162, 178.

63. Küng, *The Church*, 218–20.

64. Ibid., 222–23.   65. Ibid., 192.   66. Ibid.

67. Ibid., 195. Küng gives an elaborate survey of heretical movements, 193–97.

68. Ibid., 196.   69. Ibid., 198–203.   70. Ibid., 176.

71. Ibid., 274–76; about diversity in the New Testament Church, see Küng, *Council in Action*, 163; in the early Church, ibid., 235.

72. Küng, *The Church*, 263. For a definition and historical development of the terms "Catholic" and "ecumenical," see ibid., 296–305, 307. See also Küng's bibliographical note in *Structures*, 44.

73. Küng, *The Church*, 266–67. Küng deplores the fact that the Catholic leaders during the time of the Counter-Reformation accepted the label "Roman," because it could undermine its Catholic posture, ibid., 305.

74. Quoted by Küng in ibid., 267.

75 Ibid., 268.

76. Ibid., 313. This is one of the few locations where Küng identifies himself as an evangelical Catholic.

77. Ibid., 275.

78. Ibid., 301.

79. Ibid., 273, 275, 285. Küng apparently is not aware of Congar's

warning against the "spiritualism" of Luther and Zwingli. Congar, *Vraie et Fausse Réforme*, 384, 428; Küng is therefore accused of having a Protestant frame of reference in the official Vatican report. See Häring and Nolte, *Diskussion*, 43.

80. Küng, *The Church*, 227–30, 295–99. Also, Vatican II spoke of the total presence of Christ in the local churches, but they are "under the sacred ministry of the bishop." Abbott, *Documents of Vatican II*, 50.

80. Küng, *The Church*, 300.

82. Ibid., 318. In this section, Küng argues against the negative statement: "no salvation outside the Church" and encourages the positive statement: "salvation within the Church."

83. Ibid., 305–6.   84. Ibid., 269–70.   85. Ibid., 308–9.

86. Ibid., 271. Küng mentions four evasions of seeking Church unity; this would be the eschatological fulfillment theory, see ibid., 281–82.

87. Ibid., 269–76 on "Unity in Diversity."

88. Ibid., 241–60, a detailed discussion on "The Church and the Heretics."

89. Ibid., 248–49.

90. Quoted from Augustine's *Ennarationes in Psalmos* by Küng in ibid., 245.

91. The French Catholic scholar, Louis Bouyer, makes a similar observation: "After all churches have been declared equal . . . he attempts to maintain a certain unique role of the Catholic Church," Häring and Nolte, *Diskussion*, 53–54.

92. "Zwei Ekklesiologien?" in ibid., 158–59.

93. "Zu einer ökumenischen Ekklesiology," in *Diskussion*, W. A. Visser et al., 222–56.

94. Ibid., 166–67. Congar also uses the terms biblicism, Paulinism, or Corinthism in qualifying Küng's approach.

95. For instance, in Häring and Nolte, *Diskussion*, by Louis Bouyer, 46; by Semmelroth, 96, and by Averey Dulles, 94.

96. Congar, "Brief an Hans Küng" in *Diskussion*, 298–301.

97. See also Congar: "The Church is not to be understood from the Petrine service, but rather the Petrine service from the Church," in *Diskussion*, 173.

98. To be discussed in chap. 5, section 4 of this book.

CHAPTER V

1. "A Candid Preface" in Küng, *Infallible*, 11–30, dated "Tübingen, Pentecost, 1970."

2. Ibid., 11.

3. Hans Küng, *Truthfulness: The Future of the Church* (London: Sheed and Ward, 1968), 24; where Küng states also that this material was used for lectures at various universities in the United States.

4. Ibid., 18. Küng's books on *The Church* and *On Being a Christian* are both based on the cooperative leadership of prophet and priest. See also Küng, *Truthfulness*, 21, 109, 121, 186, and 220, on the tension between pastors and teachers.

5. Küng, *Infallible*, 20; although some cooperative theologians like Daniélou were nominated as Cardinals; ibid., 28.

6. Ibid.

7. Ibid., 29; Küng did not request authorization for his later books either.

8. Ibid., 26.

9. Küng, *Truthfulness*, 148, and *Infallible*, 19; Küng, *Fehlbar?* 323, includes also the questions of the Jews, religious freedom, the Ecumenical movement, and the veneration of Mary.

10. Küng lists the encyclicals *Ecclesiam Suam* (1963), *Populorum Progressio* (1967), Mysterium Fidei (1965), *Sacerdotalis Coelibatus* (1967), *Humanae Vitae* (1968), the papal *Credo* (1968), and the decree on mixed marriages. See *Infallible*, 25.

11. Ibid., 51–63, "Why the Pope was not convinced."

12. The statements against artificial contraception had been made by Pius XI in his encyclical, *Casti Connubii* (1930), and were confirmed by Pius XII in 1951 and 1958.

13. Küng, *Infallible*, 40; Küng seemed to assume that Daniélou formulated the text when he refers to the "Gallic" clarity of its statements, see ibid., 34 and also 22.

14. Ibid., 62, 177.

15. Küng, *Justification*, XLIII; see also Küng in Barth's obituary referring to their frequent discussion of the pope and the Petrine office, Häring and Kuschel, *Hans Küng*, 43.

16. Küng, *Council, Reform and Reunion*, 129

17. Ibid., 132.

18. In connection with the publication *Structures of the Church* (1962), Häring and Kuschel, *Hans Küng*, 173. It became an open conflict in 1970 with the publication of *Infallible? An Inquiry.*

19. Küng, *The Church*, 449.

20. Küng, *Structures*, 117 pages on the Petrine office compared with thirty-five pages on the concept of infallibility.

21. Häring and Kuschel, *Hans Küng*, 174.

22. Walter Jens, ed., *Um Nichts als die Wahrheit* (Munich: Piper Verlag, 1978), 395; and Norbert Greinacher and Herbert Haag, eds., *Der Fall*

Küng (Munich: Piper Verlag, 1980), 546. A selective English translation was edited by Leonard Swidler, *Küng in Conflict* (Garden City, N.Y.: Image Books, 1981), 627.

23. United States Catholic Conference, *The Küng Dialogue, Facts and Documents* (Washington, D.C., 1980), 218.

24. Ibid., 167.

25. Ibid., where Cardinal Höffner considers only these two issues as crucial.

26. Ibid., 174–76.   27. Ibid., 177–79, 181–83.

28. E.g.; Karl Rahner, ed., *Zum Problem Unfehlbarkeit* (Freiburg: Herder, 1971), 376. Gregory Baum, et al., eds., *The Infallibility Debate* (New York: Paulist Press, 1971), 154. Of very polemic nature is Joseph F. Costanzo, S. J., *The Historical Credibility of Hans Küng* (North Quincy, Mass.: Christopher Publishing House, 1979), 383.

29. Häring and Kuschel, *Hans Küng*, 175.

30. Küng, *Infallible*, 82.

31. Häring and Kuschel, *Hans Küng*, 175.

32. Küng states in *Infallible*, 83: "From the 'collegiality" of *all* the faithful there emerges gradually a collegiality of certain groups on ministries. . . ."

33. Küng, *The Church*, 342.

34. *The Küng Dialogue*, 172; expressed by Bishop Georg Moser in letter of 24 December 1979.

35. John Calvin, *Institutes* II, 3, 6, and II, 3, 11.

36. Küng also mentions Matthew 16:18 and 28:20 in support of his concept. See *The Church*, 342–44, and *Truthfulness*, 182–86. *Infallibility*, 181–87.

37. In Küng, *Infallible*, 68, Küng remarks that the traditional Catholic teaching "presupposes" the apostolic infallibility. While he rejects this traditional Catholic "presupposition," he himself makes a similar assumption for the infallibility of the Church.

38. Aware of this fact, Küng calls his concept "a truth of faith." See *Infallibility*, 187–90.

39. Küng, *The Church*, 464, referring to Matthew 16:18ff and Matthew 18:18.

40. Küng, *Council in Action*, 227–37. The same polarity can be seen between the councils of Trent and of Constanz; see Küng, *Structures*, 312–13.

41. Quoted by Küng in *Infallible*, 98–99.

42. Quoted in Loewenich, *Modern Catholicism*, 39.

43. Quoted in Küng, *Infallible*, 87.

44. Ibid., 99–101. An additional way of maintaining the balance between

the pope and bishops is the principle of subsidiarity instituted by Pope Pius XI in 1931; see Küng, *Structures*, 240–44.

45. Küng, *The Church*, 355.
46. Ibid., 358.
47. Küng, *Structures*, 74–92.
48. See especially Küng's section on "Conflict Situations Between the Pope and the Church," *Structures*, 249–68.
49. Küng, *Structures*, 268–319, discusses in detail the events and their implications during the Council of Constanz.
50. These are discussed in ibid., 257–63.
51. Ibid., 268.
52. J. W. McClendon, "Katholische Ekklesiologie auf evangelischer Grundlage," in *Diskussion*, 252–56; McClendon was a professor at the University of San Francisco at the time of his writing.
53. Küng devotes an elaborate discussion to this concept in *The Church*, 444–80.
54. Ibid., 344–54, gives a detailed linguistic and historical report of the development of this concept.
55. Ibid., 347.   56. Ibid., 358.
57. Although Ignatius mentions monarchical bishops in Asia Minor, he does not refer to one when writing to Rome; Küng, *The Church*, 460.
58. Tertullian applied Matthew 16 to Peter and not yet to Rome; half a century later, Bishop Stephen I applied this to his own position; Küng, *The Church*, 461.
59. Küng refers, for instance, to Romans 1:8, ibid., 461; see also 459 concerning Peter's presence in Rome.
60. Küng, *Infallible*, 182–85; Küng prefers to combine perpetuity and indefectibility maintaining that the Church will not simply continue, but rather "remain in the truth."
61. The passages are: Matthew 16:18–23, Luke 22:31–34, and John 21:15–23. These are discussed in Küng's *Structures*, 358; *The Church*, 475–76; and *Being Christian*, 498–500.
62. Küng, *Infallible*, 187; *The Church*, 322.
63. Ibid., 343–44.
64. Häring and Nolte, *Diskussion*, 221.
65. Ibid., 169.
66. "Mysterium Ecclesiae" (1973) in Walter Jens, ed., *Um Nichts als die Wahrheit* (Munich: Piper Verlag, 1978), 39. See also Häring and Nolte, *Diskussion*, 37.
67. Ibid., 203; others understood Küng the same way as Congar did, like Louis Bouyer, 49; George H. Tavard, 88; and George Dejaifve, 104.
68. This author is referring to the collection of sympathetic commentators

published and edited by Hermann Häring and Josef Nolte under the title, *Diskussion Um Hans Küng "Die Kirche"* (Freiburg: Herder, 1971), 312.

69. Ibid., 228, by Hans Diem, and 251, by Hans Riniker.

70. Published and edited by Leonard Swidler, *Küng in Conflict* (Garden City, N.Y.: Doubleday and Company, 1981), 27–31.

71. See above, chap. 4, section 1.

72. See above, chap. 5, notes 4 and 5.

73. See above, chap. 4, section 1.

74. The term "magisterium" was used during and after Vatican I to indicate the teaching authority of the Roman Catholic Church; see Küng, *Infallible*, 221–23.

75. See in addition to Küng's articles and lectures of those years, his publication *Truthfulness, The Future of the Church* (New York: Sheed and Ward, 1968), 240.

76. Küng, *Being Christian*, 177–79.

77. R. Pesch argues for a close synonymity of the terms exousia and diakonia; see "Ambstrukturen im Neuen Testament" in *Diskussion*, 141–42.

78. Küng, *Council, Reform and Reunion*, 131; *Council in Action*, 230; *Structures*, 187.

79. See Küng's detailed account in *Council, Reform and Reunion*, 140–45.

80. Küng, *Structures*, 127.

81. Küng, *The Church*, 332; see also 380.

82. Jens, *Um Nichts*, 40, 41.

83. Küng, *The Church*, 370–87.

84. Ibid., 375–79.   85. Ibid., 364.   86. Ibid., 365.

87. Translation by Küng; *The Church*, 373.

88. Ibid., 377.   89. Ibid., 378.   90. Ibid.   91. Ibid., 379.

92. Ibid., 378; also Küng, *Infallible*, 237.

93. Küng, *The Church*, 434; see also Küng, *Infallible*, 238–40.

94. Küng, *The Church*, 435; also Küng, *Infallible*, 233.

95. Küng, *Council in Action*, 159–95; see also above, chap. 4, section 3.

96. Küng, *The Church*, 383.

97. Ibid., 420–21.   98. Ibid., 383.

99. Ibid., 382–83.   100. Ibid., 413.   101. Ibid., 432.

102. Ibid., 439.

103. The informal notes were published in Häring and Nolte, *Diskussion*, 32–43. It also appeared in translation in Leonard Swidler, ed., *Küng in Conflict* (Garden City, N.Y.: Doubleday and Co., 1981), 45–56.

104. The correspondence was published and edited by the German Bish-

ops' Conference, translated by the U.S. Catholic Conference, *The Küng Dialogue, A Documentation* (Washington, D.C.: 1980), 218; additional documents, until 1980, were collected and translated by Leonard Swidler, *Küng in Conflict*, 627.

105. Jens, *Um Nichts*, 23–45.
106. Ibid., 41.
107. Robert Nowell mentions at least seven cases of which the treatment of Monsignor Ivan Illich was most notable. See Robert Nowell, *A Passion for Truth, Hans Küng and His Theology* (New York: Crossroad Publishing Co., 1981), 223–24.
108. *The Küng Dialogue*, 52–60, 69–77.
109. Häring and Nolte, *Diskussion*, 28.
110. Jens, *Um Nichts*, 79.
111. Ibid., 99–108, 142–44.   112. Ibid., 144.
113. The review is published in *The Küng Dialogue*, 146–63.
114. Häring and Kuschel, *Hans Küng*, 182.
115. Abbott, *Documents of Vatican II*, 6.
116. Ibid., 7.

CHAPTER VI

1. The German edition of *Infallible? An Inquiry* was released on 18 July 1970. The world congress for Catholic theology was sponsored by the international Catholic journal *Concilium*.
2. See Nowell, *Passion for Truth*, 245; see also chap. 1, section 3 of this book.
3. Küng, *Being Christian*, 21.
4. Ibid., 529.
5. Küng was especially annoyed that his theological friends had joined the opposition; among these were Karl Rahner and even Hans Urs von Balthasar; see Nowell, *Passion for Truth*, 283.
6. Küng, *Being Christian*, 20.
7. Ibid., 686, note 80; also his book *Does God Exist?* had to leave out these subjects; see Nowell, *Passion for Truth*, 283.
8. Avery Dulles, "Dogmatic Theology and Hans Küng's *On Being A Christian*," *America*, 1976, 341; see also John E. Burkhart in *Religious Studies Review*, 1978, 91–2; and Robert McAfee Brown, "On Being a Christian," *Theology Today*, 1977, 205–11.
9. Küng, *Being Christian*, 20.
10. Ibid., 59.
11. Hans Küng, *Eternal Life? Life After Death as a Medical, Philosophical, and Theological Problem* (Garden City, N.Y.: Doubleday, 1984).

12. Küng, *Being Christian*, 114; see also Hans Küng, *Brother or Lord, A Jew and a Christian Talk Together about Jesus* (Glasgow: Collins, 1977).
13. Based on E. H. Erikson, *Identity and the Life Cycle* (New York: W. W. Norton, 1959); discussion in Küng, *Being Christian*, 70–79 and in Küng, *Does God Exist?*, 459–61.
14. Küng, *Does God Exist?*, 459.
15. Ibid., 560.
16. Küng, *Being Christian*, 64–65; see also his interview in Häring and Kuschel, *Hans Küng*, 148.
17. Küng, *Does God Exist?*, 465. For a discussion of this blending of trust and rationality see Küng, *Being Christian*, 68–79.
18. Küng, *Being Christian*, 71, 73.
19. See chap. 1, sections 1 and 3 of this book. Originally Küng wanted to use his Hegel material for a dissertation at the Sorbonne in Paris, then for an introductory address at the University of Munich. His publication thus far has no English translation; the German title is: *Menschwerdung Gottes. Eine Einführung in Hegel's theologisches Denken als Prolegomena zu einer künftigen Christo logie* (Freiburg: Herder, 1970).
20. For evidences of the emphases mentioned see Küng, *Menschwerdung*, 262, 268, 298, 404, 430, 455, and 492; for a survey of Küng's work on Hegel see Nowell, *Passion for Truth*, 245–57.
21. The German term used is *aufheben;* Quinn translates this word as "canceled" on 59 and as "cancels and preserves" on 83. Küng discusses Hegel's use of this term in *Menschwerdung*, 245–50. For a discussion of Küng's usage of Hegel's dialectic see Matthew L. Lamb in *Religious Studies Review*, 1978, 93–99.
22. See Küng's statement in *Being Christian*, 36–37: "We stand therefore . . . for an unbiased *open-mindedness* for what is modern, extra-Christian, non-Christian, human, and for relentless criticism of our own positions . . . on the one condition that there is no sellout of the Christian substance."
23. For instance, Walter Kasper, "Christsein ohne Tradition?" in Von Balthasar, *Diskussion*, 19–34.
24. For instance, Joseph Ratzinger, "Wer verantwortet die Aussagen der Theologie?" ibid., 7–18.
25. Like Karl Barth, Küng criticizes the use of the adjective "Christian" for schools, political parties and cultural associations; see his discussion in *Being Christian*, 119–26.
26. Ibid., 123.
27. Ibid., 157; see also Joseph Ratzinger in Von Balthasar, *Diskussion*, 11: "The historical Jesus . . . becomes the criterium of being a Christian."
28. Küng, *Being Christian*, 141; on 138 Küng also mentions Wolfgang Borchert and the authors of *Jesus Christ Superstar* and *Godspell*.

29. Ibid., 135.   30. Ibid., 136.

31. Küng observes that since 1953 Käsemann turned away decisively from Bultmann's mythological interpretation of the New Testament sources; ibid., 157, 626.

32. Ibid., 134.

33. See "History and Faith's Certainty," ibid., 155.

34. See "Justifiable Faith," ibid., 161–65.

35. Ibid., 83, 133, 140; and Häring and Kuschel, *Hans Küng*, 115, 147–48.

36. See "The Christ of Dogma" in Küng, *Being Christian*, 129–33 and "Interpretations of the origin," ibid., 436–50.

37. Ibid., 131.

38. See especially Alois Grillmeier S. J., "Jesus von Nazaret—'Im Schatten des Gottessohnes'?" in Von Balthasar, *Diskussion*, 60–82; according to Grillmeier, the classical creeds were not the result of Hellenistic philosophy.

39. The Jesuit scholar José Gomez Caffarena comes to Küng's rescue by stating: "In my reading, therefore, Küng says 'yes' to Nicea and Chalcedon, but it is a conditional 'yes' given from the original kerygma," in Häring and Kuschel, *Hans Küng*, 122–23.

40. The sociological context of the gospel is discussed in Küng, *Being Christian*, 35–36, 133–38, 177–80, 554–56; for his sociological orientation Küng refers to Max Weber and Emile Durkheim a.o., ibid., 62–64. Cardinal Döpfner accused Küng of reducing faith to the level of mere church politics, see U.S. Catholic Conference, *The Küng Dialogue*, 103.

41. Küng, *Being Christian*, 29; see also 35 where the two contrasting qualities are "collaboration" and "traditionalism," or 180 where "political realism" is contrasted with "authoritarianism." Küng articulates his general criticism on 36, "This (R.C.) Church has sinned more than other churches against human fellowship . . . it has refused dialogue with Christians . . . with its own 'loyal opposition,' . . . it has condemned . . . the conclusions of the natural and historical sciences." Also the World Council of Churches shares in the sins of the establishment, 29; see also ibid., "Criticism of the Church," 517–21.

42. Ibid., 179.   43. Ibid.

44. Küng simply rejects the danger of using anachronisms, ibid., 177 and 183.

45. For a brief bibliography on the Zealots, see ibid., 631, note 1.

46. Küng discusses political theology, ibid., 43–51, 180–91, 554–70; he prefers the term "social-critical theology" for his own position, 35.

47. See "Revolution," ibid., 183–85.

48. Ibid., 187.   49. Ibid., 190.   50. Ibid., 189.

51. See "Emigration?" ibid., 192–204.

52. Küng has an elaborate bibliography on the Essenes and the Qumran, ibid., 633–34.

53. Küng refers with appreciation to Reich's ideas; ibid., 59–60, 134–35, 192.

54. Ibid., 195.   55. Ibid., 200.

56. On the parallels of Pharisaism and ecclesiastical legalism, see ibid., 201–11, 240–48.

57. Ibid., 203.

58. Ibid., 204–5, 241–44; the term "accommodation" may be a better translation for the German term *Kompromiss*.

59. Ibid., 201.

60. See "The Devout," ibid., 202–4, where Küng refers to the "works of supererogation" used in Catholic moral teaching. Küng sees the beginning of penitentiary practices already in Matthew's account of the Sermon on the Mount, 247.

61. Küng, *Council, Reform and Reunion*, 99; also see chap. 7, section 4 of this book.

62. Küng, *Being Christian*, 211.

63. Küng uses the technical term: "das Koordinatenkreuz," ibid., 211.

64. See "Misunderstood cross," ibid., 573–76, see also 517–29.

65. The good theologian is called the "serious theologian," ibid., 83–88, 122, 144; he is to be distinguished on the one hand from the "court theologian," see 35, 180, 183, 202; also called "jurist-theologians," see 178, 248; on the other hand he is to be distinguished from the "modernist theologian," see 37, 519. The serious theologian will help the responsible lay person gaining a "justifiable faith," 161. The prophetic function of the theologian had already been described in Küng, *Structures of the Church*, 89; see also chap. 4, section 2 of this book.

66. Küng, *Being Christian*, 29; see 168 in connection with the need for toleration of the Jews.

67. See "The Challenge of Modern Humanisms," ibid., 25–56; on the failures of Humanism see 37–49.

68. Ibid., 31.

69. Küng warns repeatedly against a "sellout" of Christian principles for the sake of humanitarian programs; ibid., 32, 37, 122–25.

70. Ibid., 254; Küng wrote 63 pages on the identity of God's cause and man's well-being, 214–77.

71. Ibid., 30–31, 189, 570

72. Ibid., 253; the challenge of radical humanism is presented 530–36.

73. See "Relativized traditions, institutions, hierarchs," ibid., 252–55; see also 278–300.

74. Ibid., 253.

75. See "A Church?" ibid., 283–86.

76. See "The Advocate," ibid., 291–94. The German text uses the term "Sachwalter" which also can be translated "representative." Küng was severely criticized for introducing this term at the expense of the concepts "Son of God" or "mediator"; see Alois Grillmeier, "Jesus von Nazaret— 'Im Schatten des Gottessohnes'?" in Von Balthasar, *Diskussion*, 60–82; also 87–90; see also the "Declaration of the Conference of German bishops on the book *Christ Sein*, Nov. 17, 1977." in U.S. Catholic Conference, *The Küng Dialogue*, 133–40.

77. Küng, *Being Christian*, 293.

78. See "Against discouragement," ibid., 527–29.

79. See "The other dimension," ibid., 57–88; see also 214–26.

80. Ibid., 42, 47; Küng mentions T. W. Adorno, Ernst Bloch, Jürgen Habermas, M. Horkheimer and Herbert Marcuse.

81. See chap. 3, section 2 of this book.

82. Küng rejects both Albert Schweitzer's "consistent eschatology" and C. H. Dodd's "realized eschatology," see Küng, *Being Christian*, 221.

83. Ibid., 224; Küng endorses the theology of hope by Jürgen Moltmann, see 608, note 15.

84. Ibid., 225.

85. See especially ibid., 222 where Küng states in a variety of ways the relation between present and future. Although Jesus was "under the spell of the Apocalyptic movement" (181), his message should not be interpreted apocalyptically (211).

86. Hans Küng, *Freedom Today* (New York: Sheed and Ward, 1966), 1–40.

87. See "Action" and "Solidarity" in Küng, *Being Christian*, 255–77.

88. Quotes from ibid., 235; Jesus' testimony was addressed to John the Baptist who had some similarities to the Qumran community, according to Küng, 181–82. While Küng does not consider the miracle stories as valid medical accounts (229), he neither discounts the healing ministry of Christ (237).

89. See "Even enemies," ibid., 258–62; Küng rejects Nygren's radical distinction between *eros* and *agape*.

90. Ibid., 262; Küng does not discuss the social involvement by Fransciscans, Cistercians and other orders.

91. See "True radicalism," ibid., 262–77.

92. Küng has several sections carrying the term radical, ibid.: e.g. "Apolitical radicalism" (192), "True radicalism" (262), "Being Christian

as Being Radically Human" (554). The opposite concepts are "relative" and "compromise" which occur equally frequently.

93. Legalistic Pharisaism is discussed, ibid., 201–11, 238–52, 271–77.

94. Ibid., 527; see also "No natural law," 238–40; "Moral compromise," 204–5.

95. See "Not a pious legalist," ibid., 206–8; the Scripture passage discussed is Mark 2:27.

96. Ibid., 251.

97. See "God's will instead of legalism," ibid., 241–4.

98. For a brief but good bibliography on the subject of "metanoia" see ibid., 642, note 5.

99. Ibid., 242.   100. Ibid., 243.

101. See "The meaning of the Sermon on the Mount," ibid., 244–48.

102. Ibid., 242.

103. For the socio-political implications of the Gospel see ibid., 337–39. His colleague, Hans Urs von Balthasar, accused Küng of reducing theology to a sociological issue, see *Diskussion*, 86.

104. About the relation between cross and resurrection see Küng, *Being Christian*, 396–410, also 287, 334, 398.

105. Ibid., 400.

106. See "Sacrifice?" ibid., 424–27, where Küng discusses Romans 6:10 and Hebrews 7:27, 9:12, and 10:10.

107. Ibid., 427.

108. See "The conflict," ibid., 278–342.

109. Ibid., 278.

110. See "Provocative on all sides," ibid., 211–13; see also 272, 278, 328, 335. On this point Küng agrees with Eduard Schweizer, see 212 and 635, note 42.

111. Ibid.; on 328 Küng refers to "the system," on 339 to "the Law."

112. Ibid., 337; Küng refutes any support the political theologians may want to draw from the false accusations against Jesus, see 338.

113. See "Interpretations of death," ibid., 419–27.

114. On Anselm's interpretation see ibid., 422; also, Küng talks about divine initiative in the event of the atonement, see 422, 425.

115. Ibid., 391; see also "Representation" 389–92; also "Slain for us," 421–24. For a critical analysis see Hans Urs von Balthasar, "Jesus als Stellvertreter" in *Diskussion*, 87–90.

116. Küng, Being Christian, 425; see "Sacrifice?" 424–27.

117. See "The criterion," ibid., 381–89.

118. Quotations from ibid., 382.

119. Küng gives a series of modern nomenclatures for Jesus Christ, namely: God's "mandatory," "plenipotentiary," "advocate," "spokesman," "representative," "deputy," and "delegate," see ibid., 390.

120. Avery Dulles, S. J., "Dogmatic Theology and Hans Küng's 'On Being a Christian'," *America*, 1976, 341.
121. Samuel Sandmel, *Religious Studies Review*, 1978, Vol. 4, 101.
122. Küng, *Being Christian*, 358; see "The ultimate reality," 356–61.
123. See "Origin of faith," ibid., 370–75.
124. See "The appearances involve vocation," ibid., 376–79.
125. See "Clarifications," ibid., 349–56.
126. Ibid., 358.
127. See chap. 6, section 1 of this book.
128. See "Legends," pp. 361–70 and "Honorific titles," pp. 384–89 in Küng, *Being Christian*.
129. Ibid., 360.
130. See "By faith alone," ibid., 402–10; Küng argues for an agreement between Jesus and Paul and refutes the opposite opinions of Nietzsche, Overbeck, Barth and Bultmann.
131. See "Beyond fanaticism and rigidity," ibid., 399–402.
132. Ibid., 577–78; see "Understood cross," 576–81.
133. Ibid., 410. Küng does have limited sections on the doctrines of the inspiration, the Holy Spirit, and the Trinity, but does not integrate these in his presentation of the Christian faith; see ibid., 463–78.
134. See "Misunderstood cross," ibid., 573–76, also 428–36.
135. See "The great mandate," ibid., 502–9 and "Social relevance," 554–70.
136. Quoted by Küng, ibid., 551.
137. Ibid., 575–76.
138. Ibid., 282, 486; see "Charisms, offices, ministries," 484–88.
139. See "The pluriform Church," ibid., 478–502; also chap. 5, section 4 of this book.
140. See "The practice of the Church" in Küng, *Being Christian*, 514–29.
141. See "Determined Church," ibid., 508–9 and "criticism of the Church," 517–21; the latter section is a literal reproduction of the gravamina listed by 33 R.C. theologians in 1972, see 679, note 11.
142. Ibid., 528.
143. See "Liberated for freedom," ibid., 581–90.
144. Ibid., 588; see also note 21 above.
145. See note 13 above.
146. Küng, *Being Christian*, 547–48; see "The criterion for deciding what is Christian," 540–53.
147. Ibid., 601; see Küng's proposals for humanitarian policies in "Suggestions," 590–602.
148. Ibid., 400.

CHAPTER VII

1. Küng refers to the concept used by K. Erlinghagen, *Katholisches Bildungsdefizit in Deutschland* (Freiburg, 1965).
2. Küng gives no source for his information; see Küng, *Does God Exist?*, 117.
3. Ibid., 9, Küng also mentions the condemnations of Giordano Bruno, Campanella and Copernicus.
4. Ibid., 10.   5. Ibid., 9.
6. See, for example, Küng's apology for Descartes, ibid., 16–19, referring to his death "in complete submission to God's providence"; see also 122–25.
7. See: "Science and the question of God," ibid., 122–24.
8. On 8 October 1977; for its content see Häring and Kuschel, *Hans Küng*, 181–82 and Nowell, *Passion for Truth*, 311–16.
9. Häring and Kuschel, *Hans Küng*, 181.
10. Described in Küng, *Does God Exist?*, 95–101; on Wittgenstein see 93–95, 502–8; for a bibliography on the Vienna Circle see 711, note 21.
11. Ibid., 94; Küng observes that the Vienna Circle misrepresented Wittgenstein's thought since "being silent" does not entail a rejection of inexpressible transcendental reality.
12. Ibid., 95–96, see also 31–33.
13. Popper is presented as the theorist who definitively refuted the theory of Logical Positivism, see ibid., 101–6; on Thomas S. Kuhn see Küng, *Does God Exist?*, 106–15.
14. Ibid., 115–25, 181–88, 324–39 and 415–24.
15. This involves a new interpretation of the doctrines of man's original state and of original sin; it would also include mythological concepts like those of angels and demons; ibid., 116–17.
16. Ibid., 124.
17. For the numerical figures see Nowell, *Passion for Truth*, 316.
18. See "Renée Descartes," Küng, *Does God Exist?*, 3–41.
19. Ibid., 7.
20. For bibliographical data see ibid., 703.
21. Descartes attempted in a modern way a reduction of the sciences to mathematics; see ibid., 7, 29–33.
22. See chap. 1, section 2 of this book; Henri Gouhier wrote *La Pensée religieuse de Descartes* (Paris, 1924); his other publications on Descartes are listed in Küng, *Does God Exist?*, 704.
23. Küng points to his Catholic education, his pilgrimage to Loreto, his faithful profession of Catholicism among Protestants, and to his death in complete submission to God; see *Does God Exist?*, 16–17.
24. Küng uses the term "Stockwerktheorie," see ibid., (German edition),

60; the translator renders it "the two-floor theory," see Küng, *Does God Exist?*, 21, 38; Nowell, *Passion for Truth*, 317, translates it by "the two-tier theory."

25. Küng gives details of the Greek world picture and of the static concept of God; see Küng, *Does God Exist?*, 36.

26. Küng mentions the Jesuit scholar F. Morandini; ibid., 705, note 67.

27. See chap. 4, section 2 of this book.

28. Küng, *Does God Exist?*, 6, 16; see also Hegel's evaluation of Descartes, 15.

29. Küng is well aware that Protestantism has not suffered from "religious alienation" to the degree the Catholics have; ibid., 117, 235.

30. See "Blaise Pascal," ibid., 42–92; bibliographical data on 706, note 2.

31. Quoted by Küng, ibid., 50.

32. Ibid., 49.

33. Quoted by Küng, ibid., 57–58; the words are based on the Scripture passages Exodus 3:6 and Matthew 22:32.

34. Ibid., 58.

35. The translator renders "Bollwerkstrategie," ibid., (German edition), 94, by "solidly defensive strategie," ibid., 70.

36. Ibid.   37. Ibid., 82.

38. Ibid., 83; these ascetic practices prepared the way for humanistic atheism, according to Küng.

39. See chap. 6, section 2 of this book.

40. Küng, *Does God Exist?*, 88–89, about the relation between Protestantism and Catholicism; see also chap. 3, section 5 of this book.

41. See "God in the World: G. W. F. Hegel," Küng, *Does God Exist?*, 128–69; this section is a summary of Hans Küng, *Menschwerdung Gottes*, see also chap. 6, note 19 of this book.

42. Father Klein called Küng's attention to Hegel during the early fifties, then Küng wanted to apply his research towards a Ph.D degree at the Sorbonne in Paris; in 1959 he had hoped to use his material as an inaugural address for the university of Münster; finally it was published under the title *Menschwerdung Gottes;* see note 41 above.

43. Küng, *Does God Exist?*, 149.

44. Ibid., 134, 185–86.

45. See "Postatheism," ibid., 138–42, where Küng mentions that also Luther used the phrase "God is dead."

46. Ibid., 162.

47. See "The God of Evolution: Pierre Teilhard de Chardin," ibid., 171–81.

48. Ibid., 173.

49. Küng adopts this term in *The Church*, 297; on 313 he uses the term "Evangelical Catholicism."

50. Küng endorses the unity of faith and reason in Hegel; see Küng, *Does God Exist?*, 148, 182; he also praises Hegel for his overcoming of the Greek concept of God, 183.

51. Küng did not integrate the socio-religious options in both publications, even though he states that both volumes are "mutually complementary and . . . merge smoothly one into another," ibid., XXIII.

52. Ibid., 156.   53. Ibid., 189.

54. See "God—A Projection of Man? Ludwig Feuerbach," ibid., 191–216.

55. Ibid., 207.

56. See "God—Wish or Reality?," ibid., 208–10.

57. Ibid., 213.

58. See chap. 6, section 2 of this book on the Essenes.

59. See: "God—A Consolation Serving Vested Interests? Karl Marx," ibid., 217–61.

60. Ibid., 244; see also 228.

61. Ibid., 254; see also 240–41 referring to Pope Leo XIII who warned against the *plague* of socialism.

62. See "Critique of the critque," ibid., 252–61; the heading in the German edition is "Kein Zurück hinter Marx," which assigns a more decisive role to Marx than the English translation.

63. "Is religion a human fabrication?," ibid., 244–47.

64. When Marx was chief editor of the liberal-democratic paper, *Die Rheinische Zeitung*, ibid., 255.

65. Ibid., 259.

66. Häring and Kuschel, *Hans Küng*, 180; for this reason Küng is against any militant form of Liberation theology; see Küng, *Being Christian*, 555–65.

67. See "Promise without fulfillment," Küng, *Does God Exist?*, 249–52.

68. See "God—An Infantile Illusion? Sigmund Freud," ibid., 262–323.

69. For publications by and about Freud see Küng's detailed bibliography, ibid., 733, notes 1, 7 and 9.

70. See "Adler and Jung on religion," ibid., 288–94.

71. See "The importance of religion for Jung, Fromm, Frankl," ibid., 316–23.

72. Ibid., 307.   73. Ibid., 308.   74. Ibid., 336.

75. Quoted by Küng from Fr. Nietzsche, *Die Fröhliche Wissenschaft*, ibid., 352; see 371 for the remainder of the quote.

76. Ibid., 352–424; for a detailed bibliography on books by and about Nietzsche see 742–43.

77. Ibid., 360.

78. Ibid., 374–80, 391–97; because of these principles Nietzsche's philosophy is also called "Vitalism."

79. Quoted by Küng from Fr. Nietzsche, *The Antichrist,* ibid., 407.

80. See "Consequences of private nihilism," ibid., 410–12.

81. Ibid., 423.

82. See "Fundamental Mistrust or Fundamental Trust," ibid., 442–46.

83. See "Transcending man: Ernst Bloch," ibid., 483–89; on Jörgen Habermas, 579–81; on Theodor W. Adorno and Max Horkheimer, 323–27, 489–91; Adorno and Horkheimer founded the Frankfort School of critical theory of sociology; for an extensive bibliography on the relations between Christianity and Marxism see 731, note 107; and Herbert Marcuse, 559–61.

84. Quoted by Küng from Max Horkheimer, *Die Sehnsucht nach dem ganz Anderen* (Hamburg, 1970), ibid., 490–91.

85. Terms and quotes from "Longing for the wholly other," ibid., 489–91.

86. "The universal claim of scientific thought? Karl Popper," ibid., 101–6, see also 440–41; his major supporter was Hans Albert, discussed on 334–37; the latter wrote a critical refutation of Küng's claims; see Hans Albert, *Das Elend der Theologie, Kritische Auseinandersetzung mit Hans Küng* (Hamburg: Hoffmann und Campe, 1979).

87. K. R. Popper, *The Logic of Scientific Discovery* (London: 1959); Vienna, 1934.

88. See note 10 above.

89. The terms are quoted in Küng, *Does God Exist?*, 103 and 440; Küng quotes Popper saying, "We do not know; we can only guess," 105.

90. Instead of a rational *argument* Küng presents a "rational justifiable" *alternative* between "to be" or "not to be," ibid., 453, or between life and death, light and darkness; see "Fundamental Mistrust or Fundamental Trust," 442–553.

91. Ibid., 449.

92. Ibid., 464; Küng's pragmatic argument is based principally on William Stegmüller; see "Fundamental trust as basis of science," 461–65.

93. Ibid., 442.

94. Küng uses Erik H. Erikson, *Identity and the Christian Life Cycle* (1959), see: "Fundamental trust as a lifelong task," Exdrich Bollnow, Küng, *Does God Exist?*, 452, 458.

95. See: "The Fundamental Alternative," ibid., 438–41.

96. Ibid., 453.

97. Ibid., 71–73; other existentialists discussed are Jean-Paul Sartre, 432–35, and Martin Heidegger, 491–502.

98. Ibid., 435; see "Experience of Freedom," 435–38; for a further discussion see "Gift and Task," 451–53, and "Belief in God as Gift," 575–76.

99. Ibid., 436.

100. Ibid., 450; see also "Belief in God rationally justified." 573–75.

101. See "Fundamental trust and religious faith"; Christian faith has priority over other forms of human experience and thought. See e.g., 647: "Faith and its children—religion, philosophy and world vision—are indispensable to any civilization."

102. See "The one God and the many Gods," ibid., 624–27, and "The nameless God in the Buddhist religion," 594–96.

103. Ibid., 585–86; see also "The God with a name," 621–22, and "God of the philosophers—God of the Bible," 664–66.

104. As did theologians Hendrik Kraemer, Karl Barth, Emil Brunner and Friedrich Gogarten, ibid., 609.

105. Here Küng follows Arnold Toynbee and the American philosopher William E. Hocking, ibid., 609.

106. Ibid., 627.

107. See "Is God a Person?," ibid., 631–35.

108. See "Does God intervene?," ibid., 642–49, and "Miracles," 649–54.

109. Küng incorporates the theory of "quantum mechanics." See "God and his world," ibid., 627–31.

110. Ibid., 652.

111. Küng discusses the "Big Bang" theory in "What was there at the beginning?," ibid., 635–42; and the "pulsating" or "oscillating" and "entropy" theories in "What comes at the end?," 654–59.

112. Ibid., 639.

113. See "Knowledge of God by reason: Vatican I," ibid., 510–14, and "Controversy on natural theology," 518–28. Küng briefly discusses the classical proofs of God's existence, 529–36.

114. Ibid., 518.

115. See "Knowledge of God by faith: Karl Barth," ibid., 414–18, 525–28.

116. Ibid., 536.

117. Ibid., 666. Küng wants to complement Kant's "Practical reason" by Hegel's dialectic: see 544. For an evaluation of Kant, see "More than pure reason: Immanuel Kant," 536–51.

118. Küng exhorts his readers strongly to Christian social action. See "Fundamental trust as the basis of ethics," ibid., 465–73; see also 578–83, 659–64, 691–93.

119. See note 13 above.

CHAPTER VIII

1. For the sequence of events see Nowell, *Passion for Truth*, 326–57.

2. The papal "Declaration by the Sacred Congregation for the Doctrine of the Faith on Some Major Points in the Theological Doctrine of Professor Hans Küng" was edited and translated by Leonard Swidler, *Küng in Conflict* (Garden City, N.Y.: Doubleday, 1981), 384–88; a detailed explanation of the papal declaration was also delivered to Küng on 18 December by an emissary of the local bishop, Msgr. Georg Moser; published in U.S. Catholic Conferences, *The Küng Dialogue*, 180; the crucial document by bishop Georg Moser was issued on 30 December 1979; reprinted in Swidler, *Küng in Conflict*, 418.

3. By Frits Groeneveld, "Hans Küng over de kerk en de vrijheid van geloof en wetenschap" in *N. R. C. Handelsblad* (Rotterdam, March 28, 1981) 23; Swidler adds that Küng suffered "chest pains and other ominous symtoms," Swidler, *Küng in Conflict*, 440.

4. For a discussion on the Pope's attitude see Peter Hebbelthwite, *The New Inquisition? The Case of Edward Schillebeeckx and Hans Küng* (New York: Harper & Row, 1980).

5. The text in U.S. Catholic Conference, *The Küng Dialogue*, 180–81.

6. The correspondence and exchange of statements is best documented by Norbert Greinacher and Herbert Haag (eds.), *Der Fall Küng, Eine Dokumentation*, (München: R. Piper Verlag, 1980); this anthology covers the crucial period of 1978 until 10 April 1980; the best anthology in the English language is by Swidler (see note 2 above) covering the complete period of 1968 until the summer of 1980; the same period is covered by the official documentation by the United States Catholic Conference, *The Küng Dialogue*.

7. Küng accepted a compromise agreement on 8 April 1980, allowing him to remain director of the Institute for Ecumenical Research and, in addition to filling the chair for ecumenical theology, he was to remain part of the Doctorate and Habilitation committee; see Swidler, *Küng in Conflict*, 503–6.

8. Ibid., 398, 425; see also documents on "World Protest," 511–85.

9. Ibid., 587–89.

10. See "Why I Remain Catholic" (18 January 1980) in Greinacher,

Der Fall Küng, 171–79; also his final letter to the pope on 25 August 1980; no text available, see Swidler, *Küng in Conflict*, 607.

11. See "Where I Stand" in *Pacific School of Religion Bulletin* (Berkeley, Ca., Vol. LIX, No. 1, January, 1981), 1–9; see also Küng's letter to Pope John Paul II, 30 March 1979, in Swidler, *Küng in Conflict*, 370–77.

12. Häring and Kuschel, *Hans Küng*. 182.

13. Hans Küng, *Art and the Question of Meaning* (London: SCM Press LTD., 1981), 55.

14. Ibid., 54.

15. E. Kübler-Ross, *On Death and Dying* (New York: Tavistock Publ., 1970).

16. Hans Küng, *Eternal Life? Life After Death as a Medical, Philosophical, and Theological Problem*.

17. Ibid., XV.   18. Ibid., 231–32.   19. Ibid., 233–34.

20. "The *Leitmotiv* of Küng's work is his passionate anxiety to preach the gospel . . . ," Nowell, *Passion for Truth*, 18.

21. See "A Theologian-Historian's Evaluation," Swidler, *Küng in Conflict*, 609–13.

22. See Häring and Kuschel, *Hans Küng*, 173; also chap. 4, section 1 of this book.

23. See chap. 1, section 3 of this book.

24. See chap. 6, section 1 of this book.

25. See Häring and Kuschel, *Hans Küng*, 162–63.

26. Frits Groeneveld, "Hans Küng over de Kerk," 23.

27. See chap. 6, section 4 and chap. 7, section 4 of this book.

28. Hans Küng, *Signposts for the Future* (Garden City, N.Y.: Doubleday, 1978), 94.

29. See chap. 7, note 49 of this book.

30. Küng, *Signposts for the Future*, 117.

31. See chap. 3, section 3 of this book.

32. Küng, *Signposts for the Future*, 100; see also "Participation of the Laity in Church Leadership and in Church Election," 132–54. See also chap. 4, section 3 of this book.

33. Küng, *Signposts for the Future*, 143.

34. Ibid., 157; see also "Women in Church and Society," 155–59.

35. See "What is the Essence of Apostolic Succession?," ibid., 95–101.

36. Ibid., 97; Swidler, *Küng in Conflict*, 610; and chap. 5, section 4 of this book.

37. See chap. 4, section 2 of this book, especially notes 39 and 40.

38. See chap. 7, section 2, note 24 of this book.

39. See chap. 2, section 3 of this book.

40. Küng *Signposts for the Future*, 118.

41. Küng's early endorsement of Luther still included some reservation concerning his personal interpretation of the Scriptures, see chap. 3, section 2 of this book; in recent years Küng considered this personal approach a point of strength. "It was only the new awareness brought by the Reformation to the Christian faith . . . which made possible a constructive discussion with the modern age," Küng, *Does God Exist?*, 70.

42. Quoted by Küng in his early years in *Council, Reform and Reunion*, 62 as well in his recent publication "An interim appraisal" in *The New York Times*, 19 October 1979, 35.

Bibliography

I. Works by Hans Küng

Art and the Question of Meaning. Translated by Edward Quinn. London: S.C.M. Press, 1981.

Brother or Lord? A Jew and a Christian Talk Together about Jesus. Hans Küng and Pinchas Lapide. Translated by Edward Quinn. London: Fount Paperbacks, 1977.

The Changing Church: Reflections on the Progress of the Second Vatican Council. Translated by Cecily Hastings et al. New York: Sheed and Ward, 1965.

The Church. Translated by Ray and Rosaleen Ockenden. New York: Sheed and Ward, 1967. Paperback edition, Garden City, N.Y.: Doubleday & Co., 1976.

The Church—Maintained in Truth. Translated by Edward Quinn. New York: Seabury Press, 1980.

Consensus in Theology? A Dialogue with Hans Küng, Edward Schillebeeckx, and David Tracey. Edited by Leonard Swidler. Philadelphia: Westminster Press, 1980.

The Council in Action: Theological Reflections on the Second Vatican Council. Translated by Cecily Hastings. New York: Sheed and Ward, 1963.

The Council, Reform and Reunion. Translated by Cecily Hastings. New York: Sheed and Ward, 1961.

Does God Exist? An Answer for Today. Translated by Edward Quinn. Garden City, N.Y.: Doubleday & Co., 1980.

Eternal Life? Life after Death as a Medical, Philosophical and Theological Problem. Translated by Edward Quinn. Garden City, N.Y.: Doubleday & Co., 1984.
Freedom Today. Translated by Cecily Hastings. New York: Sheed and Ward, 1966.
Infallible? An Inquiry. Translated by Edward Quinn. Garden City, N.Y.: Doubleday & Co., 1971.
Justification: The Doctrine of Karl Barth and a Catholic Reflection. Translated by T. Collins et al. New York: Thomas Nelson & Sons, 1964.
Menschwerdung Gottes, Eine Einführung in Hegels Theologisches Denken. Freiburg: Herder Verlag, 1970.
On Being a Christian. Translated by Edward Quinn. Garden City, N.Y.: Doubleday & Co., 1976.
Signposts for the Future (essays). Garden City, N.Y.: Doubleday & Co., 1978.
Structures of the Church. Translated by S. Anastasio. New York: Thomas Nelson & Sons, 1964.
That the World May Believe. Translated by Cecily Hastings. New York: Sheed and Ward, 1963.
Truthfulness: The Future of the Church (essays). New York: Sheed and Ward, 1968.
What Must Remain in the Church (essays). Glasgow: Collins, 1977.
Why Priests? A Proposal for a New Church Ministry. Translated by Robert C. Collins. Garden City, N.Y.: Doubleday & Co., 1972.

II. WORKS EDITED BY HANS KÜNG

Küng, Hans et al. *Council Speeches of Vatican II.* Glen Rock, N.J.: Paulist Press, 1964.
Küng, Hans (ed.). *Papal Ministry in the Church.* New York: Herder and Herder, 1971.
Küng, Hans. *Theological Meditations.* New York: Sheed and Ward, 1966.
Küng, Hans and Jürgen Moltmann. "Ecumenism," an annual issue of the International Journal *Concilium.* New York: Seabury Press, 1965.
Tracy, David with Hans Küng and Johann B. Metz. *Toward Vatican III. The Work That Needs to Be Done.* New York: The Seabury Press, 1978.

III. WORKS RELATED TO HANS KÜNG

Congar, Yves M. J. (O.P.). *Vraie et Fausse Réforme dans l'Eglise.* Paris: Editions du Cerf, 1950.

Costanzo, Joseph F. (S.J.). *The Historical Credibility of Hans Küng.* North Quincy, Mass.: Christopher Publ. House, 1979.

Greinacher, Norbert and Haag, Herbert (eds.). *Der Fall Küng.* München: Piper Verlag, 1980.

Häring, Hermann and Kuschel, Karl-Josef. *Hans Küng. His Work and His Way.* Translated by Robert Nowell. Garden City, N.Y.: Doubleday & Comp., 1980.

Häring, Hermann and Nolte, J. *Diskussion um Hans Küng. "Die Kirche."* Freiburg: Herder Verlag, 1971.

Hebbelthwite, Peter. *The New Inquisition? The Case of Edward Schillebeeckx and Hans Küng.* New York: Harper & Row, 1980.

Jens, Walter (ed.). *Um Nichts als die Wahrheit. Deutsche Bischofskonferenz contra Hans Küng—Eine Dokumentation.* München: Piper Verlag, 1978.

Kirvan, John J. (ed.) *The Infallibility Debate.* New York: Paulist Press, 1971.

Nowell, Robert. *A Passion for Truth. Hans Küng and His Theology.* New York: Crossroad Publ. Comp., 1981.

Rahner, Karl (ed.). *Zum Problem Unfehlbarkeit. Antworten auf die Anfrage von Hans Küng.* Freiburg: Herder, 1971.

Richardson, James Earl. *The Küng-Rahner Debate over Infallibility.* Pasadena, Ca.: Fuller Theological Seminary, 1973.

Ryan, Michael D. *The Contemporary Explosion of Theology:Langdon Gilkey, Hans Küng. Teilhard de Chardin.* Metuchen: Scarecrow Press, 1975.

Swidler, Leonard (ed. & transl.). *Küng in Conflict.* Garden City, N.Y.: Doubleday & Comp., 1981.

United States Catholic Conference (ed. & transl.). *The Küng Dialogue. Facts and Documents.* Washington D.C.: 1980.

Von Balthasar A.O. *Diskussion über Hans Küng's 'Christ Sein.'* Mainz: Matthias-Grünewald-Verlag, 1976.